Northwestern University
STUDIES IN *Phenomenology* &
Existential Philosophy

Prefatory Note

THE CHAPTERS OF THIS BOOK REPRODUCE, IN somewhat expanded form, a series of six lectures, entitled "Christianity and Existentialism," which were delivered to the general public on the Evanston Campus of Northwestern University from October 11 to November 15, 1961. The purpose of these lectures is to explore, in a series of dialectical discussions, the impact of the existential viewpoint in philosophy on religious thought, particularly in its relevance to Christian philosophy.

Contents

Christianity and Existentialism

I / Faith as Existential Choice

(THE PUNIC FATHERS)

NEARLY ALL HISTORIANS of contemporary intellectual history now date the revival of religious philosophy and the several neo-orthodoxies it has carried with it to the impact of the thought and character of Sören Kierkegaard.[1] Kierkegaard is *the* prophet of Christianity in our epoch. Like a Jeremiah or a John the Baptist living in the arid desert of the nineteenth century, the century of the destruction of the forces of the spirit, Kierkegaard announced the inescapable and irremediable death of the institutions of Christendom in order that Christian faith might be reborn. One episode of his extraordinary life has, in particular, gripped the contemporary imagination: the ten months from December, 1854, through September,

[1] Cf. William Barrett's introduction to "Neo-Orthodoxy" in *Philosophy in the Twentieth Century* (New York, 1962), II, 617–27.

1855, when he feverishly penned his last testament to the Christians of Denmark, the *Attack on Christendom*. Having spent himself in this one last extravagant effort, which he himself termed the work of a madman, he collapsed and died, alone and at peace. Like a prophet of the Old Testament he *acted out* in these last months the judgment of rejection he had delivered verbally on the official Church.

> I do not call myself a Christian, do not say of myself that I am a Christian. . . . Yes, I know it well enough, it sounds almost like a sort of madness, in this Christian world where all and everybody is Christian . . . that there, in this Christian world, one says of oneself, "I do not call myself a Christian," and especially one whom Christianity concerns to the degree that it concerns me. . . . I do not call myself a "Christian" . . . , but I am able to make it evident that the others are that still less than I.[2]

It would be fatuous to compare Kierkegaard's rejection of the Christian name with all those statements of "Why I Am Not a Christian" that have been penned by other nineteenth- and twentieth-century philosophers. Kierkegaard rejected the name "Christian" in the way Socrates rejected the name "wise man"—in order, as he wrote, "to keep the ideal free." His whole life's task was to define what it is to be a Christian, and he discovered, in the face of the institutions of Christendom, that a Christian is not something one *is* but something that one may, per-

[2] *Attack on Christendom*, trans. Walter Lowrie (Princeton, 1946), pp. 282–83.

haps *become* at the cost of great personal risk, anguish, and effort. It is not a *status* which one acquires once and for all by an "official act," which then distinguishes the Christian forever, in spite of himself, from the rest of humanity so that we can neatly distinguish "Christians" from "non-Christians" simply by looking up the registers of membership in a given Church organization. Christianity is not a club of initiates. It is not a *state* but a *lived effort,* a task that will remain eternally incomplete, which is to say that it will never be completed this side of eternity. In short Christianity is a type of *experience,* a dimension of life-in-the-world, an intention *to do* something in the world, a vision that is at the same time an action. Christianity is not a science to be studied, but an *activity* that involves the would-be "Christian" in the whole of his being and alters his very existence.

The supreme category in Kierkegaard's thought is religious *faith.* By attempting to understand this category, which can never be fully understood or explicitly thematized, we will approach as closely as possible to the real meaning of Kierkegaard's rejection of Christendom. If one were to define faith merely as *belief,* whether in the "doxic" sense of Hume and Husserl or in the sense of an intellectual assent to a series of divinely revealed propositions, one would distort the most profound intention of Kierkegaard's thought. For the essential motive force of this thought is its attack on the Hegelian rationalization of Christian experience. By the time Kierkegaard entered upon the nineteenth-century intellectual scene, Hegel's system had been cheerfully adopted by leading Christian theologians to express the "truths" of the Christian religion. The underlying supposition of this procedure, accepted without criticism by the Church theologians, is that religious experience, Christianity itself, can be expressed as a systematic intellectual construction. It is this attitude towards Christianity that Kierkegaard categorically rejected; theologians were making Christianity into an "official doctrine" rather than a way of life, a lived activity. If there is such a thing as *Christian* philosophy, he says in effect, it must be based on the denial of the very possibility of Christian *philosophy*. The rationalist attempt to make Christianity into a body of "truths," into a type of systematic intellectual science *to be taught* rather than *lived* prior to any objectifying thought, this is what Kierkegaard rejected. In so doing he reasserted an experience of Christian faith which, we shall see, was also recognized in other periods of Christian history and described in circumstances very different from Kierkegaard's Denmark. Perhaps the first expression of this experience occurs in the Punic Fathers, particularly in Tertullian, who is, after Kierkegaard, the most eloquent witness to this experience of faith in the Christian tradition. Our discussion will begin with Kierkegaard and then lead back to his earliest predecessors.

However, if we define religious faith *as action rather than knowledge,* we must not make the mistake of making Kierkegaard into a simple-minded activist, another Victorian social reformer. The action which *is* faith for Kierkegaard is not a dispersal of the self in "doing good" to others. This sense of action is not excluded, but it must flow from a more "ontological" faith rooted in the prior conversion of the *self*. There are many ways to "love" the world, but only one of them comes from *faith*.[3]

Bultmann and Tillich have defined this conception of faith in terms of a pre-rational or pre-cognitive self-understanding.[4] Here everything depends on what one means by *self-understanding*. For Kierkegaard, the Socratic, in search of the "definition" of what it is to be a Christian, we can assuredly admit the necessary *turning to self* which is the underlying source and condition of experience. But this must not be understood exclusively as a solipsistic turning within, as if "knowing oneself" and "affirming oneself" in faith did not also, necessarily, involve the transcendent reality without which no experience of self would be possible. A similar qualification must be made concerning the term *understanding* which is, nevertheless, the least misleading term we can use in this connection. We have already excluded fully thematic, cognitive awareness of the propositional form as adequate to express the foundational experience of faith. Faith is prior to any *knowledge*

[3] I cannot agree with Walter Lowrie that Kierkegaard's attack on official Christianity involved the contravening of the *sola fide* of the Lutheran tradition. Kierkegaard is *the* Protestant of Lutheranism, not only in the sense that he protested against it but also, and primarily, in the sense that he testified for a conception of *sola fide* which is certainly more Lutheran than Tridentine. For Kierkegaard, no more than for Luther, can "true religion" be adequately defined in terms of social action and medical missionaries. This is not the sense of *action* involved in Kierkegaard's notion of faith. Cf. Walter Lowrie, Introduction to *Attack on Christendom*, p. xvii.

[4] Cf. Rudolph Bultmann, *Kerygma and Myth* (New York, 1961), pp. 208-11.

about the activity of faith itself or its contents. In fact it is as unwise to speak of the "contents" of faith in this sense as it is to speak of the "contents of consciousness" as if consciousness were a container of some kind. This does not, however, exclude the reflective examination of the action of faith *after the fact,* so to speak, in an Augustinian sense. It is in this sense that one can begin to speak of Christian *philosophy.* But faith itself is an operating understanding which precedes and conditions all rational reflection concerning it. Abraham *understands* what he must do without being able to *say* it either to Sarah or to Isaac or to Eleazer, and this ineffable understanding *is* his faith.

In this very preliminary effort at grasping the Kierkegaardian notion of religious faith which it was, he believed, his mission to proclaim, and which is at the origin of modern religious existentialism, we can summarize our results as follows: (1) faith is doxic *belief* only in the sense that it is not subject to scientific demonstration and that it is impervious to complete rational or logical justification; (2) it precedes and conditions any attempt at fully rationalizing or even fully thematizing its object or its "content"; (3) it is an *action,* not only in the sense of a practical *doing,* but primarily in the sense of a *becoming* by which the self is established in a dynamic relationship of continual self-transcendence towards itself, the world, other men and God; (4) it can be correctly though imperfectly defined as an operating, pre-cognitive *self-understanding* in which and by which the man of faith is unconditionally related to "the transcendent" and "the eternal"; (5) it is, therefore, *absolute* in the sense that it is self-originating and self-justifying.

But, up to now, we have neglected one element, the essential one. Kierkegaard is the founder and inspiration of contemporary religious existentialism. This Christian existentialism erupted into the world of the late nineteenth and early twentieth centuries as a new and radical break with the past—as a *philosophy of the absurd*. If philosophy is the work of reflecting on experience, Christian philosophy is the work of reflecting on *the absurd,* the experience of Christian faith. "The Absurd," or the human experience of the absurd, is one of the fundamental categories of existentialist thought, whether Christian or non-Christian. We are concerned here particularly with "the absurd" as it is revealed in religious experience. But it is, first of all, necessary to say one or two things about the *meaning of the absurd,* for the absurd *has* meaning.

Like all fundamental words the word "absurd" carries many meanings and is used to designate in a confused way very disparate phenomena, not all of which are listed in our dictionaries under this word. We can limit ourselves here to two of these insufficiently distinguished meanings, the first of which involves the use of the word "absurd" to designate *the nonsensical*. This is a very old category in Western philosophy and goes back—as a technical philosophical term—to Zeno and Aristotle, the founders of Western logic. In their usage the word "absurd" signifies a self-contradictory expression or an expression that hides within itself an inner contradiction (hence all the logical arguments of Zeno are forms of "reduction to absurdity"). But even in logic we must be careful of misusing this word. Husserl has pointed out the dangers of confusing the simple non-sensical (*Unsinn*) with the countersensical or self-contradictory (*Wiedersinn*), the latter of which does not designate a simple lack of meaning.[5] To turn from logic to life, Merleau-Ponty in his series of essays edited under the title of *Sens et non-sens* and in his *Phenomenology of Perception* has shown the richness of *the nonsensical* in human experience and behavior. The evolution of a human life or the development of history involves a complex dialectic of sense and nonsense, of meaning and non-meaning, not only because we find much that is due to chance, much that is botched, much that is unfulfilled in human existence, but primarily because much of what we experience as meaningless or absurd does *not yet* have meaning. If man is the source of history and if it is human consciousness which confers meaning on being, the meaning of human existence itself is essentially ambiguous, shifting, dynamically unstable, an inextricable mixture of sense and nonsense.

But this is not the place to attempt an analysis of the category of "the absurd" in all its ramifications. We are concerned primarily with focusing attention on the *lived experience* of the absurdity of existence which is revealed occasionally, at certain moments in our lives: at the times when we are led by some inner necessity of thought and reflection out of our everyday, taken-for-granted life in the world, to pose the *question of existence* in all its stark reality—"What does it mean?" "Why does something exist

[5] Cf. Edmund Husserl, *Logische Untersuchungen*, II, IV, 12, and Marvin Farber, *The Foundation of Phenomenology* (Cambridge, 1943), p. 325.

rather than nothing?" In a world in which everything *could be* other than it is, why do we have *this world*? Our utter inability to answer such questions or even to understand what is asked when they are stated in this way brings us into the presence of the absurdity of existence. In this sense of the word, the one which has chiefly preoccupied the existentialists, the word "absurd" is pregnant with meaning: it signifies the experience which leads us to pose the problem of the meaning of existence. In this sense we can follow a recent author in his apt definition of the absurd as "the intrinsic questionability of all order."[6]

In our ordinary, everyday existence we do not question the world or the order of the world. We take it for granted. On the pre-reflexive, on the pre-philosophical level there is no problem of the absurdity of existence. The world is what it is; we are what we are; we unquestioningly go about our affairs without asking "philosophical" (i.e., "stupid") questions. But underneath this unquestioning acceptance of our world and intrinsic to our unreflected existence lies the *possibility* of questioning it, for our lives are intrinsically *questionable*. The absurd is, therefore, a continual dimension of our existence; it is always *there*, whether we choose to advert to it or to ignore it, always capable of erupting to the surface of our awareness and of imposing itself as a problem which cannot be avoided. There come moments in experience when the question of the meaning of existence imposes itself, and these moments are frequently "religious" moments. For a philosopher these are the

[6] Maurice Natanson, "Causation as a Structure of the Lebenswelt," *The Journal of Existential Psychiatry*, I (1960), 358.

moments when he *begins to wonder* about what everyone else takes for granted, about what he ordinarily takes for granted.

What is it that we ordinarily take for granted? That the world is basically an orderly and rational place following rational laws, in which everything is causally connected with everything else, and that *everything* somehow has a meaning and fits into some rational scheme. We may not *know*, like Hegel, what the totality of this scheme is, but we live our lives on the unreflected assumption that there is one and that existence is "meaning-ful." In short, on the level of ordinary, commonsense existence, we do not need or employ any systematic concept of "orderliness" in the world; it lies there rather as an implicit structure of the life-world that is ordinarily not thought about, which, in fact, does not *bear* much thought, which is simply taken for granted in the interests of good mental health and practical necessity.

When I prepare, for instance, to take a long trip, I buy my tickets in Chicago, perhaps months in advance of my departure, for various destinations, to be reached on determined days, let us say in Europe and Africa. I may also, then, buy tickets for passage by sea across the English Channel and the Mediterranean Sea, on ships I have never seen, operated by companies of which I have no previous knowledge, whose personnel are there waiting for me on the appointed days, to take care of me, clean my cabin, answer my questions, bring me my meals and permit me a wide selection of wines I have never tasted. I pursue my journey from city to city, using the tickets I have so "thoughtfully" provided for myself, with a simple trust in the enormously complex social order which infallibly makes my tickets valid on just the days I want to use them, to meet just the connections I have planned to meet, at just the piers in just the seaports I have designated, and so on. A whole army of anonymous fellow men are engaged in doing things they do every day, speaking foreign languages, and, in general, "thoughtlessly" making my journey possible, from stop to stop, all the way back to Chicago. But what complete faith in the orderliness of the world supports all this! I am sustained at every minute by a host of commonsense beliefs concerning the viability of this social order which I need not and probably never could make fully explicit. I simply live my life *within the horizon* of such commonsense life-world beliefs.

But there come moments—in reflection—when these typical commonsense beliefs reveal themselves as "human" beliefs, as the result of "human" constructions, when the world itself is seen as the result of human activity. Or, if we leave the world of social order for that of science, the moment will come when all those supposed "natural" laws reveal themselves as crude human attempts to give a meaning to the world and that, *in itself,* "nature" is perfectly indifferent to human science. All of our commonsense notions about the world are capable of suddenly revealing themselves in their full contingency. If the orderliness of the world is the result of human-activity-in-the-world, it *could* all be otherwise than it is. This is what is *meant* (i.e., intended), at least in part, in an *experience of the absurd.* It is the experience of the radical contingency of human life, of human social institutions, of human science, of all order. It is through the experience of the absurd, the questionability of all order in the universe, that men have been led most frequently to pose the problem of religious faith.

The philosophy of the absurd, as a religious philosophy, is associated in modern philosophy with the name of Kierkegaard. Though he lived and died over a century ago, it is only in our own day that his thought has become a dominant intellectual force in Western philosophy, and thus modern philosophers tend to see existentialism as something radically *new*, a new style of philosophizing, even an entirely new experience. But if we look at the matter somewhat more closely, we will see that a Kierkegaardian view of human experience, of history, of thought, has been a perennial element in the *religious experience* of the world and that it has been attested to by persons of very diverse historical periods. The absurdity of human order reveals—to the Christian—more than a problem; it reveals a mystery. The absurd cannot be conquered by reason; it can only be answered by faith, by the decision to begin somewhere, to invent what is not yet given, to create in order to know. Here we have the final element, and the essential element, in Kierkegaard's notion of *faith*: it is *an answer to the absurd*, and, as such, it is itself an *absurd answer*. "A paradoxical and humble courage is required to grasp the whole of the temporal by virtue of the absurd," he writes, "and this is the courage of faith."[7] That frightening "by virtue of the absurd" rings as a refrain through the writings of Kierkegaard and gives them their

[7] *Fear and Trembling*, trans. Walter Lowrie (Princeton, 1952), p. 70.

prophetic rhythm and unity.

We can now pose the question of whether the Kierkegaardian conception of faith is meant to confront Christianity with a *new* problem, the result of the challenge of existentialism as a twentieth-century philosophy, or whether it is something more fundamental still. Recently we have seen the origins of existentialism pushed back to the Slavophiles and the Pochvenniki, to Dostoevsky, to Pascal, then to Augustine, to Plotinus, even to Plato, and finally to Hinduism. It is doubtful that the roots of this movement can be pushed back much further, since with early Vedantic philosophy we are already approaching the prehistoric period of human life and thought. After having begun by thinking of Kierkegaard as a radical innovator, some of our contemporaries are now surprised to find existentialist themes in the philosophy and literature of nearly every epoch they examine. Is existentialism then a *perennial philosophy*? And is Kierkegaard to be deprived of his originality as the initiator of a new style of thought?

Here we are concerned exclusively with *Christian existentialism*, and perhaps two remarks should be made to help situate the question. First of all, existentialism in its relation to Christian philosophy cannot be considered simply as a contemporary challenge, another attack from without that would require a redefinition of the Christian message in the categories of Heidegger's *Daseinsanalyse*, for instance, to make it acceptable to the twentieth-century mind or to revitalize it as a social force. The problem of Christian existentialism as it is being stated here is situated much more deeply than that; it concerns the very raison d'être of Christian man.

Secondly, it would seem that Christianity is not to be singled out among the world religions as somehow more or less challenged by "existential" problems than, let us say, Judaism or Buddhism or Hinduism. A study of historical Christianity can, at best, provide us with a paradigm case for the wider problems of the phenomenology of religious experience. The lesson we have learned from the few scattered and incomplete studies of this nature which have been undertaken up to the present time is that the religious dimension of experience is apparently the most deeply rooted of all and the most difficult to disclose in its specificity. Imperfect as they may be, existential and phenomenological analyses of ethical, aesthetic, social, and political experience are much further advanced than similar studies in the realm of religious experience. Because the moods, feelings, emotions, motives, desires, impulses, attitudes, and actions (in the widest sense) designated under the ambiguous name of "religious experience" penetrate all the levels of the conscious and pre-conscious behavior of man, any hope of coming to grips with them as a totality or of thematizing them in a unified philosophy of religion must remain a distant hope.

In any case the aim of this essay is more modest. It is to attempt to trace, in bold strokes, one of the roots of the Christian "irrationalism" of which Kierkegaard has become the modern symbol. The roots of this irrationalism go very deep, and there is no better place to begin than at the beginning, to go back close to the foundations of Christian thought, to the age of the martyrs and fathers, to a group of documents which, despite its richness and diversity, bears witness to a specific experience of

Christian life at once distinctive and consistent, the writings of the early Punic Fathers. The North African Christian writers from Tertullian through Lactantius, Cyprian, and numerous others up to Augustine form a school of thought which had its own development, its own specificity, and which—through the Latin medieval Augustinian tradition—has continued to influence the development of Western religious thought up to the present. One of the themes of this literature is the experience of the absurd which discloses the mystery of existence and thereby dictates the nature and necessity of man's absolute response to God in faith. The result of this study will not be to impugn the originality of Kierkegaard but to see him in relation to the first Christian philosopher of the absurd, Tertullian, and perhaps to suggest, in the manner in which they "defined" Christian faith, an *historical meaning*, even a unity, which is one of the perennial elements of the Christian experience.

What is this extraordinary African Church and what does it mean to Christian philosophy? First of all, it was a *Mediterranean* Church, conditioned by its place as the most protected, most isolated, perhaps most prosperous of the Roman provinces under the Empire—*Africa Proconsularis*. It had the smallest standing army, was the least affected by the civil wars that periodically erupted in the Empire, and was the last to feel the weight of the barbarian invasions. In a sense North Africa at the time of the coming of Christianity was the most *Roman* of the Roman provinces and the most *pagan*. There is a softness about the North African climate and the cultures it has supported that has been mentioned by many authors, ancient and modern. Fertile soil, profuse vegetation, continual sunshine, an open horizon and proximity to the sea predispose the North African to a worship of natural forces, to an uninhibited sensuality. This southern shore of the Mediterranean is at once a sensually delightful and a cruel place in which to live. Plants, animals, and men grow fast and mature early along this rich shore, but the searing desert winds and the implacable noontime sun creep up from behind and take their daily revenge. The sea is friendly and invites to lightheartedness, but the desert with its savage beasts and unknown terrors constantly and implacably threatens to reclaim its rights at the least faltering of human vigilance. Springtime and youth are short; dessication, decay, and death are perhaps more *visible* and more present here than anywhere else on earth. It is no accident that the modern atheistic exponent of the philosophy of the absurd, Albert Camus, was a native North African. In his *Noces* he paints in powerful pagan strokes a picture of the North African way of life where everything is born for pride and life and where everything is given to be taken away: uninhibited joy in the natural powers and profuse life of youth, resignation to fate, acceptance of death as a natural fact, and *without hope*.[8]

[8] It is worthwhile calling attention to the religious desperation as well as the pagan frolic of Apuleius' *Golden Ass* —"a story of sin and redemption," says Michael Grant, *The World of Rome* (New York, 1960), p. 198. Apuleius was a North African who lived and wrote from A.D. 125 to 180. Tertullian and Apuleius should be read together. For a general introduction to the Roman culture of the North Africa to the Punic Fathers, cf. Gilbert Charles-Picard, *La civilisation de l'Afrique Romaine* (Paris, 1959).

It was in this North African province of the Roman Empire that Western Christianity first came to the age of maturity. Like its climate the North African Church was precocious. It was more Roman than Rome itself. Whereas in Rome the educated classes, including the first Christian theologians, spoke and thought and wrote in Greek, the North Africans invented and gave to posterity the first Christian *Latin* vocabulary. From the days of Tertullian to the time of Augustine this province of the Empire resisted Hellenization, and there is something in the Punic mind that is profoundly hostile to Greek rationalism and Greek culture in general. Christianity spread more rapidly here than it did in Rome or Italy as a whole, and it was here that the moral and intellectual contest with paganism reached its highest pitch. To be a Christian in the age of Tertullian was "to live dangerously." Just to read the list of his writings reveals this; the theme of unrelenting opposition to the official religion of Rome, the duty of facing martyrdom, is the unifying theme of his writing: *Against the Heathens, To the Martyrs, On Idolatry, Concerning Flight Under Persecution* are some of the titles, and it was a fellow North African, Lactantius, who wrote the moving *On the Deaths of the Persecutors.*

These books give us an arresting picture of the intense moral conflict in which the Christians had engaged their surrounding fellow beings. It was a mortal as well as a moral conflict—a fight to the death. And it is with irony and defiance that the North Africans lay down the challenge: "Ave Caesar, morituri te salutant!"

Crucify us, torture us, condemn us, destroy us! . . .
Yet your tortures accomplish nothing, though each is
more refined than the last; rather, they are an entice-
ment to our religion. We become more numerous
every time we are hewn down by you: the blood of
Christians is seed.[9]

If we compare the *Apologies* addressed to the
Roman Emperors by Tertullian and other North
Africans with those more restrained, philosophically
sophisticated, eirenic apologies penned in Greek by
such writers as Justin or Aristides or Athenagoras,
for example, we are impressed by the defiance, the
intransigence, even the violence of the Africans.
Here we have an instructive contrast. In his *Dialogue with Trypho* Justin gives us the story of his
conversion. As a young man he had tried out all the
fashionable bourgeois philosophies of the day—
Stoicism, Peripateticism, Pythagoreanism, and finally Platonism—without finding in any of them
the way of life he was seeking, until one day a
chance meeting with a simple old man by the sea-
shore opened up for him "a love of the prophets"

[9] Tertullian *Apologeticum* 50, trans. E. M. Daly, *Fathers
of the Church*. Under Septimius Severus (A.D. 193-217), the
first native North African to become Emperor, the North
African Church underwent a period of savage persecution
to which Tertullian bears witness in his *Ad Scapulam*
(Scapula was Proconsul at Carthage during the persecution
of 211–213) and other writings. "The cry to set the lions
upon us is raised every day," he writes in *De Spectaculis*
27, and, in *Apologeticum* 40, he lists some of the pretexts
on which Christians were attacked. The contemporary
Passio Perpetuae et Felicitatis, perhaps also written by Tertullian, is a story of North African ferocity and Christian
strength in this period.

and of "those men who are friends of Christ," and he resolved to study the writings of the Christians. The words he chose to describe his conversion to Christianity are striking:

> I found this philosophy alone to be safe and profitable. *Thus and for this reason I became a philosopher,* and I could wish that all men were of the same mind as myself, not to turn from the doctrines of the Savior.[10]

Justin then put on the distinctive garment worn by Greek philosophers, the pallium, and visited the Imperial cities where philosophy was most cultivated to teach Christianity as the new and true philosophy. When he ultimately settled in Rome, he could think of no more noble way of living the Christian life than that of setting up a school of philosophy where he could write refutations of other schools of Greek thought and pen urbane apologies to the Emperor, Antoninus Pius, and the Roman Senate. For this he was nevertheless ultimately executed in the reign of Marcus Aurelius, as a member of that race of *pessimi exempli* then disturbing the Empire, the Christians.

We can even say that this Greek-speaking, thoroughly cosmopolitan and Hellenized citizen of the Empire is the first clear representative of that long line of converted Greeks who attempted to baptize Greek philosophy and to build bridges between Athens and Jerusalem. Justin's response to the Christian message was to create the science of theology, and he was the forerunner of all those who have "thought" themselves into the Church, of all

[10] *Dialogue with the Jew Trypho* 8; italics mine.

those for whom faith includes *gnôsis*. Becoming a Christian did not in the least entail the loss of his earlier admiration for the figures of Plato and Socrates or his belief in the efficacy of philosophical reason. Later on, as the great Alexandrian school of philosophy gradually became Christian, such proto-theologians as Clement and Origen continued in this tradition and, on the basis of middle-platonic and neo-platonic philosophy, began the fateful attempt of "demonstrating" the "true philosophy" as the Christian religion was now to be called.[11]

Tertullian's conversion to Christianity included no such desire. The Christian "rationalism" launched by Justin and the Greek apologists and so eagerly taken up by the philosophically sophisticated Greek Christians of Tertullian's day (especially his contemporaries Clement and Origen) appealed to him even less than their attempts to build bridges between the Christian and pagan communities within the Empire.[12] Tertullian would have

[11] Cf. Clement of Alexandria *Stromata* II. Extreme forms of this "Alexandrian" tendency resulted in the purely "gnostic" theologies of early Greek Christianity and, in the Middle Ages, in the Latin Neoplatonism of John Scotus Erigena who is credited with the forthright statement: "No one enters heaven except through philosophy."

[12] The great pagan attacks on Christianity such as the *True Word* by Celsus, Porphyry's fifteen books *Against the Christians*, or Hierocles' *To the Christians* were philosophically reasoned treatises which argued that Christian faith is an insult to reason. While Alexandrians, like Origen, would attempt to answer such arguments, a Tertullian would ignore them as having missed the point. Christianity *is* an insult to reason. In his apologetical works Tertullian is more ready to threaten than to reason with his adversaries—as he does in the *Ad Scapulam* when he warns the

none of it. The divine Socrates whom Justin called "a Christian," and whom centuries later Erasmus was to enroll in the catalogue of the saints, Tertullian dismisses as only "a corruptor of young men." Aristotle is "the miserable Aristotle," inventor of the science of dialectics, "the art of building up and pulling down, an art so far-fetched in its conjectures, so harsh in its arguments, so productive of contentions—embarrassing even to itself, retracting everything, and really treating of nothing."[13]

It is not only that Tertullian's attitude towards Greek philosophy as a means for understanding the Christian faith was not favorable. Faith destroys the need for philosophy altogether.

What indeed has Athens to do with Jerusalem? What concord is there between the Academy and the Church? What between heretics and Christians? Our instruction comes from the porch of Solomon, who

Proconsul not to "fight with God." "We who are without fear are not seeking to frighten you, but we would save all men if possible by warning them not to fight with God" (*Ad Scapulam* 4, trans. S. Thelwall, *Ante-Nicene Fathers*). The μη φεομαχειν, in Greek in the text, is meant to recall Peter's warning to the Sanhedrin (Acts 5:39). When Tertullian does undertake to refute a philosopher, as in his book against Hermogenes for instance, his arguments are taken mainly from Scripture or Christian experience and are seldom strictly philosophical.

[13] *De praescriptione haereticorum* 7, trans. P. Holmes, *Ante-Nicene Fathers*. Cf. *Apologeticum* 46: "Adeo quid simile philosophus et Christianus? Graeciae discipulus et coeli?" However, Tertullian was easier on Seneca: "Seneca saepe noster" (*De Anima* 20).

himself taught that the Lord should be sought in simplicity of heart. Away with all attempts to produce a mottled Christianity of Stoic, Platonic and dialectic composition! We want no curious disputation after possessing Jesus Christ, no research after enjoying the gospel! With our faith we desire no further belief.[14]

This is more than a mere tendency to blame all aberrations from faith on pagan philosophy, a tendency which can be found in *any* of the Fathers of the Church. It is an attack on philosophical reason itself. This "ardens et eristicus vir," as Saint Jerome called Tertullian, turned his not inconsiderable dialectical talents to the destruction of philosophy itself. Though his own education certainly included the reading of philosophy and though his own thought moves largely within the intellectual framework of Roman Stoicism, from which he takes many key terms and ideas, he nevertheless strenuously fights against the suggestion that Christianity is a philosophy. In the last chapters of his *Apology* he argues against those of his contemporaries who, convinced of the truth of Christianity, are content to adopt it as a kind of philosophy. Sacred Scripture, he asserts, is the "treasure chest" from which "every subsequent system of philosophy" has taken whatever truth it contains, only to becloud the original message with conflicting and contradictory interpretations. Philosophy, in fact, is a work of the devil, and philosophers are "the patriarchs of heretics" who have "distorted the Old Testament."[15] For

[14] *De praescriptione* 7.

[15] *Apologeticum* 47, *De praescriptione* 7, *De Anima* 3.

Tertullian Christianity is not another new philosophy, but *truth itself*, and the two are incompatible.

Another important characteristic of Punic Christianity as evidenced in the writings of Tertullian is its *ethical radicalism*.[16] Perhaps it is precisely because of the "epicurean" flavor of North African life that we find a rigorism in African Christianity which goes beyond anything reported by any other ancient Christian community of this size. The Montanists were succeeded by Christian Manicheans and then by the Donatists who preserved the spirit of African rigorism down to the very extinction of Christianity itself in these provinces. Though condemned by the official councils of the Church, it is beyond doubt that the "rigid theories" of these African sects, and the Donatists in particular, found unequivocal support in the writings of Tertullian and Cyprian and that they represented the native sentiments of the early African Christians.[17] We find in the writings of Tertullian, particularly in his later periods, and in Cyprian also, an impatience with the institutionalized policies of compromise and "laxity" of the official Church, an emphasis on the *personal* character of faith and salvation, in

[16] Tertullian has been called "the first great Puritan of the West." If we take the word "Puritan" in its original etymological as well as historical meaning, it aptly describes Tertullian, though we might better label him a *Puritan existentialist*.

[17] For the later North African Fathers Tertullian, despite his "heretical" end, always remained *the Magister*. Cyprian used to begin his day by reading from the works of Tertullian, and his influence on the others, including Augustine, was nearly as important. Cf. Jerome *De viris illustribus* 53.

short a puritan extremism which is not wholly absent even from the fully orthodox Augustine. Towards the end of his life Tertullian rejected the official Church altogether, and, according to some, he died an embittered and disillusioned old man, demanding that Christians must *actively* seek out martyrdom while avoiding it himself. According to others, he retired from this world into a heroic solitude in search of a spiritual martyrdom since his own ardent longing to testify to his faith in blood had been denied him. Of his actual end we know nothing. We must return to his writings.

In his book *On Spectacles* we see the Christian conscience at grips with the pagan world. Tertullian speaks of the public games in the circus, the gladiatorial contests with wild beasts in the amphitheater, the athletic games in the stadium, and the other public ceremonies of the Roman world with emotion.[18] Only Augustine's description of the gladiatorial shows in Rome equals it in moral feeling. It is difficult for us to understand the grip that the Roman thirst for blood and the Roman worship of

[18] It is typical of Tertullian's "African" style that he concludes his book *On Spectacles* with the scene of the final judgment situated in an amphitheater, where the saved will "rejoice and exult" over the torments to be meted out to their former persecutors on earth: the Emperors will groan, Proconsuls and philosophers and poets will tremble at the sight of the avenging Christ, tragic actors will finally be worth hearing and athletes and charioteers will finally be worth seeing as they are tortured to death by flames! "What praetor or consul or quaestor or priest with all his munificence will ever bestow on you the favor of beholding and exulting in such sights?" (*De spectaculis* 30, trans. R. Arbesmann, *Fathers of the Church*).

the spectacular held on the Western Mediterranean world of that time—or to understand what it could mean for the Roman citizen of Africa to convert to Christianity, to renounce the games, the theater, service in the legions, attendance at civic ceremonies, public office, and in effect to renounce citizenship in *the City* of this world, Rome, to become citizens of "another world." These are the terms in which Tertullian puts the Christian choice: a total renunciation of the Roman Empire itself in favor of a higher truth. Truly an absurd demand pushed, as Tertullian pushed it, to absurd lengths.

Here we have one of the keys of the Christian existentialism of the Punic Fathers: this was *an age of conversion*. Both of Tertullian's parents were pagans; he had risen to a prominent place in the Roman administration as a lawyer and magistrate before renouncing his career to become a Christian. Even Augustine, two centuries later, still belonged to the age of conversion. And, as he tells us in his *Confessions*, he had to experience the delights and cruelty of Carthage and Rome, to live through his period of intense anxiety in which, as he says, he could not tell right from wrong, truth from falsehood, before he could become a Christian. It was not a step one took lightly. Perhaps that is why, in our day, we meet truly existential Christianity almost exclusively in the literature of conversion. In a society in which people are officially inscribed in the rolls of the Churches at birth, in which we live in nations that are Christian "by definition," in a world where men have entrusted their consciences to "experts," in which Christian faith causes men no anxiety because its "contents" have already been officially decided and codified beforehand and we have only to look them up in scientific treatises of theology, it is impossible to experience Christianity as a converted Roman experienced it. Perhaps that is what Pascal and Kierkegaard meant when they said that, as Christians, they had still to be "converted" and *become* Christian. If one can become a Christian only after having crossed the bridge of despair, it is not only contemporary philosophers who ought to reject the title.

We can put the "existentialism" of Tertullian in proper relief by pointing out two themes which lie closest to the center of his thought and to which he returns again and again. The first and most important point concerns the primacy of faith. When Tertullian says it is necessary to live "by faith" he is not making a simple moral exhortation; he is observing an existential structure of human life. Nor does he mean, by faith, primarily the intellectual assent to a proposition taken on someone else's word, even God's. He means the total engagement of one's being in a way of life for which there is not and never can be adequate rational evidence or even an adequate rational guarantee. Faith is a decision to act before one "knows," to act, if necessary, against the evidence, against *the evident*.

The Son of God was crucified; I am not ashamed because it is shameful. And the Son of God died; it is absolutely believable because it is absurd. And he was buried and rose again; it is certain because it is impossible.[19]

[19] *De Carne Christi* 5. Some authors, such as Gilson, complain that this text has been misinterpreted and that

From the *Credo quia ineptum* of Tertullian to
Kierkegaard's "paradoxical and humble courage of

the *credo quia absurdum* (Tertullian actually used the word
ineptum, which has the same meaning) not only does not
"define the spirit of Christian theology, but its very negation." "Ever since the time of Athenagoras," writes Gilson,
"theologians have been most anxious always to establish at
least the *rational possibility* of the Christian faith. In this
sense, they have all believed because it was *not* absurd to
believe. As to Tertullian himself, even if we remember that
he was a rhetorician, it is hard to admit that he ever intended to place the criterion of truth in absurdity" (Etienne
Gilson, *History of Christian Philosophy in the Middle Ages*
[New York], p. 45). This is evident to Gilson for two reasons—namely, because to him the "absurd" means the "illogical," and, secondly, because the science of theology,
which operates exclusively within the limits of Greek logic,
cannot assimilate the "illogical." But Tertullian is speaking
of what we have called an *experience of the absurd,* defining not Christian *theology* but Christian *faith.* Gilson's protest is based on an equating of theology with faith, an equa-
tion which Tertullian would have been the first to reject.
However, in order to avoid misunderstanding, it is necessary to point out that Tertullian in his earlier works, such
as the *De praescriptione,* did follow the path of Irenaeus
and the earlier "Greek" theologians in speaking of *faith* in
terms of a fixed belief in certain more or less well defined
propositions and of establishing a *rule of faith* to determine
its exact "content." This is one meaning of "faith" in the
early Tertullian. But in his later works, particularly after
he became a Montanist, he tended to make faith more and
more into an ineffable personal experience which precedes
and prescribes any "rules." But the essential point is that
even when he spoke of the *rule* of faith, it was more in
terms of a common historical experience that ties the "be-
liever" to the historical Christ and his Apostles and Prophets
than in terms of a philosophically explicit and established
"doctrine"—as an open, developing sacred history rather
than a fixed formula of belief.

faith" which operates "by virtue of the absurd" the distance is only one of time, not of meaning. Here we have, surely, one of the constants of the Christian experience. Men *need* faith because of the incommensurability of human reason to the mystery of existence. By faith the Christian throws the whole of reality out of focus in order to refocus it in a new perspective which is its own justification. It is, Tertullian tells us, vain to try to justify the Christian style of life by relying on philosophical reason. For a choice of this kind is made first and then thought about, or rather it must be made in order that it can be thought about. The *Credo ut intelligam* of Augustine and Anselm are to be understood in this light. For the Augustinians, less hostile to philosophy than Tertullian, reason is imperceptibly given a larger role, but this does not in any way alter *the* existential fact that faith is prior to reason by an ontological as well as a temporal priority. When Augustine and Anselm later attempt to "demonstrate" the truths of Christianity, they first invite their readers to have faith. With faith, the demonstration is easy; without it, impossible.

Any attempt to analyze this Punic notion of faith further seems doomed to failure. The philosopher is not even permitted to pose his questions. It is evident, he may say, that all men must live by faith, but what is the justification for living by *this* faith? Any Christian could give answers, and Tertullian gives many of his own, among which the example of the martyrs is the most deeply felt;[20] but, ultimately, no two Christians ever give answers to this

[20] Cf. *Ad Scapulam* 5.

question that exactly coincide, and in any case their *answers,* Tertullian would say, are irrelevant. This is the "divine absurdity" of faith.

The second theme of Tertullian's Christian existentialism which may be pointed out flows very naturally from the foregoing considerations. It involves the very forceful stress put in his writings on the personal and concretely individual nature of the Christian's relation to God. Tertullian does not begin, as do the Platonists, with a dualistic theory about the body and the soul. The arguments of Plato in the *Phaedo,* he tells us, are without value. He is so opposed to Plato's view that he does not hesitate to affirm that the soul itself is corporeal, a body. In reading the philosophically confused and obtuse work which is Tertullian's *De Anima* as it progressively shows that the shape of the soul is similar to that of the body, that it is, in fact, the life-breath, that it originates with the body, grows with the body, and shares the ultimate fate of the body in the resurrection of the flesh,[21] one cannot escape the impression that Tertullian is really trying to argue for a very Hebraic, non-dualistic view of man. His main evidence is taken largely from the Hebrew Scriptures. The least that can be said is that his anthropology is an original, non-Greek approach to the subject. In his more successful, and more important, work on the *Testimony of the Soul* he realizes that the main obstacle to Christian faith is not the pagan theory of the soul but pagan education in general. He bases himself on the "natural

[21] This last point is dealt with more fully in a special treatise, *De resurrectione carnis,* and forms a sequel to the *De Anima.*

man," simple, rude, uncultured and untaught, not yet ruined by Greek education—*anima naturaliter christiana.*

He precedes Augustine in developing *psychological approaches* to God. Here there is nothing of the Greek cosmological approach, the harmony of the spheres, or wonderment at the divine order of nature. Contrary to "some of our brethren" who have not lost their taste for Greek philosophy and who attempt to show that what the pagan authors wrote about God will provide "proofs for the truth of Christianity," Tertullian asserts that nobody will find the truth about God and the soul in such laborious speculation "unless he is *already* a Christian.[22] Instead, Tertullian attempts to lead the individual (soul) to God by showing that there is an immediate and direct experience of God open to all men and that this experience reveals man's relationship to God without the need of extensive philosophical instruction. "You are not," he writes, "Christian; *for man becomes a Christian—he is not born one.*" But it is nevertheless in the "natural" experience of all men that we find "testimonies of the soul" concerning the way to God which "are as true as they are simple, as simple as they are common, as common as they are universal, as universal as they are natural, as natural as they are divine."[23] He invites his reader to return to his own religious experience as it is prior to any thought or theory about it, to *explore* his spiritual life, in order to find the Christian route to the true God. This interest in the

[22] *De testimonio animae* 1.

[23] *Ibid.* 5, trans. R. Arbesmann, *Fathers of the Church.*

psychological approach to God is common to all the African Fathers, and, on the basis of it, Augustine, as is well known, made his most original contributions to Western philosophy and theology.[24]

If we were to turn now to the writings of Augustine, we would remark, first of all, that the character of his environment seems to have changed radically since the days of Tertullian. North Africa is no longer prosperous or at peace; the standing army is as large as it is ineffectual; the overtaxed cities are being gradually depopulated; the desert is beginning to reclaim fields laboriously made fertile by Roman engineers since the days of Caesar and Augustus; life has become more rude, and settlements of Vandals are scattered among the Roman towns and villages. But, more important than this, the tables have been turned on the persecutors; Christianity is the state religion, and Augustine, as bishop, is one of the officials of the Empire. Whereas two hundred years earlier Tertullian had pleaded with the Proconsul Scapula for freedom of religion,[25] Augustine does not now hesitate to employ the Imperial police

[24] This is apparent not only in the *Confessions* and more personal works of Augustine but also in the *De Trinitate* and his other doctrinal works. It remained a constant of the Augustinian theological tradition throughout the Middle Ages.

[25] *Ad Scapulam* 2: "It is the law of mankind and the natural right of each individual to worship what he thinks proper, nor does the religion of one man either harm or help another. It is not proper for religion to compel men to religion, which should be accepted of one's own accord, not by force . . ." (trans. R. Arbesmann, *Fathers of the Church*).

against the Donatists and other heretics.[26] From being the hunted and the persecuted minority, the Christians have become the official persecutors of pagans, Jews, and even other Christians—the heretical sects. But in this confused period, during the years that preceded the final extinction of Roman power and the establishment of a barbarian kingdom, we know from the witness of Augustine that the spirit of the old Rome remained firm. Augustine was a pagan, in the full sense of the word, before he became a Christian, and the description of life at Carthage and Rome which he gives in his *Confessions* is recognizably the same world as that of the first Punic Fathers. Augustine is *not yet* a medieval. The writings of this tormented, sensitive, brilliant Roman have all the fire, all the audacity, and especially the sense of personal commitment of the earlier North Africans, and his philosophy has been aptly called "a metaphysics of conversion."[27]

But Augustine no longer feels threatened by Greek philosophy in the way that Tertullian did. When he rejects "the philosophies of the Gentiles" in the name of the only "true philosophy"—the Christian way of life—he is continuing Tertullian. But his own spiritual progress through the sects of

[26] Cf. Augustine's letters to Gildo, Boniface, and other Imperial *Comites Africae;* he lauds them when they are zealous in using their military power in the defence of religion and blames them when they show less energy. Cf. *Letters* 185, 189, and all the letters concerning the Donatists, especially the letters to the Tribunes Marcellinus, 139, and Caecilianus, 86.

[27] Etienne Gilson, *The Christian Philosophy of Saint Augustine* (New York, 1960), p. 240.

the Manicheans, the Academics, and the Platonists to Christianity enabled him to give philosophical reason, particularly in its mystical, Neoplatonic expression, its due. Augustine's thought tends towards a precarious synthesis which, while "taming" the extremism of Tertullian, keeps its inner power and vital force. Augustine's notion of faith involves a dialectical tension between *pistis* (faith) and *gnôsis* (knowledge) which is never resolved. In some sense a philosophical investigation of faith, a theology which is not a science but a "wisdom," is possible. But it is only possible for the man of faith; it comes *after* the lived experience of faith and is never adequate to the task of full rationalization which philosophy requires. There is no hint of a scientific system of faith in the works of Augustine; the understanding which follows faith is always partial, groping, subject to revision, not a solid, articulated structure like a medieval *Summa,* but a temporary crutch for the weak and inadequate human mind.

Unfortunately, we cannot trace here the development of these themes further through the history of Christian thought. We can only note, in conclusion, that this tension between *pistis* and *gnôsis,* which Augustine was able to hold in solution, was more and more accentuated by his successors until faith and reason became the two conflicting constants of medieval theology. Augustine is the ambiguous thinker who is the fully orthodox "doctor of grace" while remaining "the father of heresies."

The "Augustinianism of the right" attached itself to the early decision of the theologians and bishops of the major Christian Churches to become *didaskoloi,* teachers of systematic theology. From the beginning there have been Christians who, using the philosophy at hand, have tried to *explain* the Christian message, to systematize it, to make it into a kind of rational, orderly science. This effort probably reached its culmination and found its most perfect expression in the serene, thorough, architectonic system of Thomas Aquinas in the thirteenth century. Aquinas' first question in the *Summa Theologiae* is *Utrum sacra doctrina sit scientia*—is theology a science? The affirmative answer given to this question and Aquinas' *tour de force* in defining Christian theology as a science in the full Aristotelian meaning of the term is the keystone of his thought. When, later in the *Summa*,[28] he defines faith as an "act of the intellect," he is making explicit, in Aristotelian terminology, a decision which the early Greek Fathers had taken as early as the second century at least.

To trace the development of theology as a science of faith would be a laborious but not a difficult task since this is the conception of Christianity which has been officially favored through the centuries, and we are in possession of all the texts and documentation required. But a really good history of what we can call the "Augustinianism of the left" has never been written and would present much greater difficulty. Representatives of this viewpoint crop up in unexpected places in the annals of Christianity only to be suppressed, to disappear from view temporarily, and then to re-emerge often in more "virulent" form in different historical and doctrinal contexts. They are frequently the "heretics" or those suspected of

[28] *Summa Theologiae,* II-II, 4, 2.

heresy in their day, though many remain more or less within the mainstream of orthodoxy. We have no intention of suggesting here how such an investigation should be conducted. What seems certain is that if we now observe the history of Christianity from the viewpoint of Kierkegaard's conception of faith *as action rather than knowledge,* we find that it is not something new but that it has been one of the two constants in Christian life from the beginning. There has always been a strain of what can be called Christian "irrationalism" (which is not always to be understood as an "anti-rationalism") opposed to the strain of Christian "rationalism" in the Christian experience of the world. There have always been "philosophers of the absurd" to challenge the Church theologians in their conception of faith as knowledge and theology as science.

Certain periods and places have seen a more concerted attack on this conception of Christianity than others. We have observed the case of Punic Christianity. The period that led to the early Protestant Reform is another. Early in the fourteenth century a certain malaise came over the theologians of Northern Europe. Whereas Anselm had tried to "demonstrate" even the sublime Christian mysteries of the Trinity and the Incarnation, each following generation had found that it had to restrict the area of what could be "demonstrated" in matters of faith. Bonaventura could still easily demonstrate the existence of God and the creation of the world in time, but, for Aquinas, the creation of the world in time could "only be held on faith,"[29] and his great philo-

---

[29] *Ibid.,* I, 46, 2.

sophical demonstrations concern the existence of God and the immortality of the soul. But Aquinas is not nervous. The scholastics of the thirteenth century are in the calm possession of the truth; the papacy is supreme in Europe; the crusaders are in Constantinople and Palestine; the Moors are retreating in Spain; the Christian religion is finally about to achieve the ultimate intellectual and political synthesis; and Aquinas can devote all his intellectual energies to a rational defence and explanation of the institutions of Christendom *as they are*, even down to and including the Inquisition itself.[30]

But with Scotus, then Ockham and the Franciscan spiritualist movement, we find a gradual change of climate. Henry of Ghent opens his *Summa* of theology not with the question of whether theology is a science but with the epistemological question: "Can man know something?" Scotus is still able to demonstrate the existence of God, but he considers any demonstration of the immortality of the soul impossible. Finally, Ockham takes the step of stating that *none* of these Christian truths can be demonstrated, not even the existence of God, that they can only be believed. Together with this Franciscan spiritualist tendency goes the increasingly heard affirmation that Christian faith is not an act of the intellect but of the will, that in faith one does not *know more* but *lives differently*. It was the Ockhamist theologians of Erfurt, Prague, Tübingen, Heidelberg, and other German universities who prepared for Luther's revolt and the new sense it gave, temporarily, to the Pauline "primacy of faith."

[30] *Ibid.*, II-II, 11, 3 and 4.

In the seventeenth and eighteenth centuries, after the Protestant sects had also become official Churches with their own orthodox and scientific theologies, and after the Council of Trent had frozen the institutions of Catholicism, movements of protest appear in the form of the pietist movement in Germany, the puritan revolt in England, Pascal and the Jansenist heresy in France. To what extent these various movements illustrate a common conception of Christian life and faith depends on what one means by faith to begin with. Our original question was whether the existential view of Christianity given to us by Kierkegaard is something radically new or whether it has always been a constant dimension of Christian experience. This essay has been limited to suggesting some of the places we must look to find an answer to this question.

JAMES M. EDIE

II / Christian Rationalism

(AQUINAS, GILSON, MARITAIN)

IN THE PRECEDING ESSAY, Mr. Edie has analyzed
the thought of the early African Fathers and has
brought out certain clearly marked existential elements in their thinking. Thus they recognized the
limits of logic and objective rational analysis, they
drew heavily from the Bible in holding that faith,
not reason, is the foundation of Christianity, and
they asserted with great force that their religion is
not to be understood as a theory but rather as a way
of life. Many of Kierkegaard's guiding insights,
which have been taken over by all schools of existential philosophy, were also derived from his reading of the Bible, and Mr. Edie is certainly correct in
saying that there is a current of existential thinking
which runs through the whole history of Christian
life and thought.

This history, however, has also been strongly

marked by other influences. The most important of these is the rational theory and science which came from ancient Greece. Its most influential representative is Thomas Aquinas, later canonized by the Church, who in the thirteenth century worked out a great synthesis of Christian theology and the Greek philosophy of Plato and Aristotle. In the following pages, I shall first give a brief sketch of this rational system; second, present the claims made by living Thomists that this is, in fact, an authentic, and even the only authentic, version of existential philosophy; and, finally, I shall critically examine these claims.

Before 1200, Augustinian thinking was dominant in the philosophy and life of the early Middle Ages. Theology was the queen of the sciences, and philosophy was not sharply distinguished from it as an independent discipline. The world is governed by the Divine Trinity which, as the eternal source of all being and truth, created it in time. God is pure and changeless being; the finite creatures, created out of nothing, are composite and changeable. One of them, man, is composed of a material body and an immaterial soul, including the two highest natural faculties, reason and will. This will is capable of free choices which have instituted a peculiar human history, in which man, misusing his freedom, became the slave of sin. But with the coming of the Divine into this history, those predestined to salvation were given the means of efficacious grace. The individual person, by his will, can open himself to faith, which, insofar as it remains alive, will not rest in ignorance. It will constantly seek rather to bring all things into the light of understanding and will thus found philosophy, together with the various

sciences and arts. According to the Augustinian tradition, the manifold truths discovered by them,
coming from a single divine source, will readily fit
into the great scheme of redemption unfolded by
the Christian revelation. This was the point of
view which dominated Western Europe before the
thirteenth century when a critical development
occurred.

In a relatively short period of time, many of the
more important texts of Aristotle, which had been
preserved in the Byzantine and Arabic worlds, were
translated into Latin and made accessible to the
scholars of Western Europe. This opened their minds
to the possibility of a purely rational exploration of
the realm of nature, unfettered by any dogmas of
faith, and inaugurated a long and bitter struggle
between rational science and faith, which was in
many ways similar to that which occurred six centuries later in the nineteenth century. For some
time, the new Aristotelian texts were banned from
the University of Paris, but in spite of this, they were
widely read and profoundly influential. The com-
mentary of the Arabic philosopher Averroes was also
translated into Latin, and it introduced what we
would call today a naturalistic interpretation of the
Aristotelian texts to many Latin minds.

According to Christian revelation, the world was
created at a given time; according to Aristotle, the
world was everlastingly in motion. For an Augustinian, the individual human soul is immortal, but
no such doctrine is found in the later Aristotelian
texts which were read at this time. Augustine believed that he had a direct awareness of his own
existence in the very act, and, in his *Confessions*

and many other writings, he attempted to express and to reveal these personal experiences as he lived them through. For the Averroist Aristotelians of the thirteenth century, however, such "knowledge" was too relative and variable to be worthy of serious attention. The only way in which we can clearly know an act that we have performed is by another act that regards it as an object from a detached point of view. Speaking out of their own lived experiences of anxiety and radical choice (Biblical notions), the Augustinians held that such free choices were the turning points of our human history, deciding not only between different ways of acting but between different worlds of meaning in which individuals and societies are able to exist. For an Aristotelian, on the other hand, everything that happens, including our voluntary choices, is caused.

The cosmic order is already established, and happiness, the end of man, has been fixed by nature. Many of the things we do are forced upon us by external causes. All that we can legitimately mean by a free act is one that is determined by causes that lie within the active agent. The Averroists skillfully defended a subtle Aristotelian determinism of this kind. According to Augustine and the Christian tradition, man had lost his freedom, and was now so enmeshed in a network of sin and corruption that he could do nothing to save himself. Such a point of view is wholly foreign to Aristotelian thought. In the first place, man never had any such radical freedom to lose. Mistakes may have been made, but the end of man remains firmly established and supported by the general nature of things.

By the use of his reason which, for an Aristotelian, is a divine element in man, and by living in accordance with nature (φυσις) and reason (νοῦς), he can still hope to attain this natural end. Hence the Averroists were inspired by a great upsurge of optimism, and we find one of their leaders, Boethius of Dacia, forcefully proclaiming: "I call him a philosopher, who, living according to the true order of nature, has acquired the best and final end of man."

Thomas Aquinas grew up in the midst of this warfare of radically opposed ideologies, and he devoted all his great talents and energies to the task of bringing them together in an overarching synthesis which would do justice to the truth which he felt lay on both sides. There is no reason for disbelieving his own comment on his life work that in theology he intended to follow Augustine, but in philosophy, as was appropriate, *the* philosopher, Aristotle. Since philosophy has a way of getting involved in everything we think and do, it is not surprising that his great synthesis was weighted heavily on the Aristotelian side and that there were few Augustinians, familiar with his works, who failed to see that it was inspired by Athens rather than by Jerusalem.

We have space here, of course, only for a brief survey of the Thomistic system, in which we shall try to show that, in spite of many minor revisions, it remains essentially Greek in its feeling tone, as well as in its basic structure and principles. This is certainly true of the conception of science which guides its procedure from beginning to end. Here Aquinas follows Aristotle in defending the notion of an absolutely empty reason which can assimilate the natures of all things and apprehend the whole cosmic order from a detached point of view outside the world. This pure, theoretical knowledge receives the formal structure of things, but with the aid of the senses, it can also distinguish between the existent and the non-existent, the actual and the potential. Its function is purely passive—to absorb the forms of things as they already are and must be, and then to express them in the form of objective judgments. When functioning properly, it is never active in the sense of being original or creative. This theoretical assimilation plays an essential role even in what Aristotle called *practical reason,* for it determines the whole world frame in which the action is to take place, and sets the end. We choose and deliberate only about the means, never justifiably about the natural end.

Aquinas follows Aristotle also in referring to metaphysics, the study of being, as a divine science. Being is the most general of all concepts. It transcends the different species and the widest genera or categories, being found in them all, as well as in the individual objects of the senses and the imagination. This concept is derived from a peculiar act of abstracting from these finite objects. But since God is the cause of them all, and since there is a minimal similarity, or analogy, between a cause and its effects, even God falls under this concept. He is the highest being, its pure act, in which no element of potency, or imperfection, is to be found.

Since it is the first and widest of all concepts, being cannot be defined. In the case of finite entities, it is the act which brings them out of the imperfect state of potency and places them among things. Aside from this, Aquinas has little to say about being, though he pays it high compliments. He conceives of it as an objective presence before the mind or as the possibility of such a presence. That which cannot be brought before the mind or the senses in this way does not exist. In every finite object, we can discern a real distinction between its essence, *what* it is, and the fact of its existence, *that* it is. This means that the essence by itself is only a potency, unable to move or actualize itself. Hence all such finite entities require a cause outside themselves to explain their existence.

Aquinas, like Aristotle, was never able to understand how any finite being, even a living organism, can move itself. Hence every finite motion and every finite act which realizes a potentiality must have an external cause that is already in act. Otherwise something would happen without a reason, the cosmos would be reduced to chaos, and ultimately the law of contradiction would be violated. These rules of objective human thinking are regarded by Aquinas as ontological principles which actually govern all the events of nature and history. This consistent application of the Aristotelian causal principle leads to a strangely static conception of a universe heavily guarded and hemmed in by formal chains. Nothing can be brought into existence unless there is a definite essence already there in potency and ready to receive it. And even while it exists, it cannot move unless there are causes already there to bring it into act. In this strictly ordered cosmos, existence seems to be dealt out grudgingly and only under carefully restricted conditions.

God is the single exception. He alone can act

without restriction. In fact, he must necessarily do so, for his essence is the pure act of being, which he must be. Aquinas does not hesitate to refer to God as necessarily existent, but one wonders whether this concept is not being stretched to the breaking point in being applied to a divinity which is subject to no limitation or constraint. One feels the same doubt with respect to the other human values like goodness, intelligence, voluntary action, justice, and mercy, which, according to Aquinas, when stretched out and intensified to the maximum degree, can be truly applied to the divine being in an analogous sense. Can this be done without introducing anthropomorphic limitations and diluting the divine transcendance? Is man made in the image of this divinity, or is it not rather true, as Feuerbach suggested, that God is a great construction made in the image of man?

The existence of this infinite being, who turns out to be so strangely, one can even say, so exaggeratedly human, can be syllogistically demonstrated by the five causal arguments presented in Question 2 of Part I of the *Summa Theologiae*. From the distinction between essence and existence in all finite beings and from their resulting contingent character, their ability either to be or not to be, together with the principle of sufficient reason, which Aquinas assumes but does not state, these causal arguments follow as a matter of course. But is the act of existing always predetermined by a prior whatness? How do we know that the universe is rational? Must it correspond exactly to our habits of objective, logical reflection? Except for references to the authority of the philosopher, Aquinas gives us no answer to these questions. As Pascal noted, they make no contact with the intuitive feeling of our lived existence and are, therefore, singularly lacking in persuasive power.

From the conclusions of these causal arguments Aquinas deduces a large number of properties, or attributes, that can be truly predicated of the divine being. Thus God is simple, immutable, eternal, omniscient, omnipotent, and endowed with every perfection. He is even referred to in strictly Aristotelian terms as the unmoved mover. This Greek emphasis on immobile changelessness is hard to reconcile with the living God of Christian faith, and the cautious hemming-in of existential activity by essences and causes, as we have noted, seems out of key with the Christian conceptions of generosity and love.

While Aquinas expressed a deep sense of mystery in his famous hymns and in cryptic statements about his life work, this is not evident in his philosophical and theological writings. They are highly impersonal, objective, and abstract and convey little sense of passion or, indeed, of any human existential feeling. His God does not speak to us from remote heights far beyond our knowledge. He does not lure us on to new thoughts and creative endeavor. He seems to think very much like Plato and Aristotle, and instead of urging us to break our chains and to go on our way, he seems rather to tighten them and to admonish us to look back and stay as we were.

God has created the cosmic order of finite beings at a given moment of time, though this cannot be proved by reason. It must be accepted on the basis of revelation. The cosmos contains an element of prime matter, or potency, that is able to receive the forms of higher objects in an ordered hierarchy: first inorganic things, then, based upon them, the nature of plants, then that of animals, and finally man, the rational animal. Above him are the immaterial angels who live a purely spiritual life, either in obeying or in rebelling against the Providence of God. Man has had nothing to do with the establishment of this order. It is now finished and fixed. A given mass of matter may receive one form, and then a higher form built upon it. In this sense there may have been and still is evolution. But the species themselves do not change. Their number is fixed, and no new species can arise. Among the different causes, the formal cause ($\mu o \rho \phi \eta$) plays the dominant role. It determines the matter to be of a certain kind, the efficient cause to act in a certain way, and the final cause or fulfillment to be of a certain nature. Man has an intermediate place in this order of forms between the animals and the angels, with both of which he is apt to confuse himself. But such confusion leads only to deformation and disaster.

Aquinas says that being is very important, and he even implies in certain statements that it is more important than essence (whatness). But they are hard to reconcile with his apparently unqualified acceptance of Aristotelian rationalism and formalism. Thus in his *Treatise on Man* in the *Summa Theologiae,* he pays little or no attention to human existence in the world and makes little effort to catch the feeling and atmosphere of this existence. As he sees it, this is too confused and variable, and he follows his master, Aristotle, in holding that there is no science of the individual. His approach is basically formalistic, and he starts with a definition, not a description. Man is not a world. He is rather a material substance, or thing, in the world among other things, which is living, animal, and finally rational. No being which lacks any of these essential features is a man; any being that possesses them is human.

After dealing with this essential nature, he turns to the properties of man which are derived from it: the faculties of growth, nutrition, and reproduction from his vegetative, living nature; sensation, desire, and locomotion from his animal nature; and the faculties of intellect and will from reason, his most distinctive feature. The natural end of man, the full realization of these faculties in their proper order in accordance with reason, as we have noted, has been set by nature. The acts of man, what he actually does, are individual and variable. Hence they fall outside the scope of this treatise, which is concerned only with the universal and the necessary, i.e., the science of man. The different virtues and vices are only accidents which leave the essential human nature untouched. History itself is a series of accidents under the firm control of a divine Providence which is able to bring good out of evil. But this series of chaotic accidents is not susceptible to scientific treatment. So, unlike his theological master, Augustine, he gives it no serious, disciplined attention.

In spite of the defects we have suggested, Aquinas possessed a very penetrating and wide-ranging mind, and within the limits of his objective, rationalistic perspective, he achieved a sweeping synthesis of objective science, Greek philosophy, and widely accepted Christian doctrines which endured through several centuries and is still alive at the present time. He possessed a shrewd capacity for making fine distinctions with some basis in observation, which enabled him to bring opposed views together in a balanced way that seemed to do justice to both sides and had a strong appeal to what we call *common sense*. But his major writings lack any vital flavor of concrete exsitence and are remote from the facts of history. In his theology, it is the Platonism of Augustine rather than his Biblical thinking that he follows. In spite of many alternations and adaptations in a Christian direction, his system is a great expression of Greek rationalism.

In spite of this, certain living Neo-Thomists, noting the way in which existential philosophy seems to express the living thought of our time, have made the claim that Thomism includes within itself the essential truths of this philosophy. Thus Professor Étienne Gilson says not only that Thomism is existential but that it is the *only* authentic existential philosophy.[1] He does not go into any detail, but supports this claim by references to the basic importance of being and to the supremacy of existence over essence in the Thomistic system. M. Maritain has made the same claim and has supported it by a more sustained argument and criticism of contemporary existential thought in his book *Existence and the Existent*.[2] Let us now review

[1] "Thomism is not another existential philosophy; it is the *only* one" (Gilson, *The Christian Philosophy of St. Thomas Aquinas* [New York, 1956], p. 368).

[2] New York, 1948.

his argument and then examine it critically. This may enable us to clarify some of the novel insights which sharply distinguish the existentialist mode of philosophizing from Thomism, as well as from other traditional modes of thought.

M. Maritain agrees with Gilson that Thomism is "the only authentic existentialism" (*op. cit.*, pp. 1–2. As he explains, this is because of "the primacy which authentic Thomism accords to existence and to the intuition of existential being" over essence (p. 2) and because of the many defects he finds in contemporary existentialism, meaning primarily the existentialism of Sartre. M. Maritain thus thinks of existentialism as a point of view which accepts the traditional Thomistic distinction between essence and existence, and then as against some Thomists who became essentialists, it follows St. Thomas in giving a certain priority to existence. But he holds that it fails to achieve this aim because of other departures from rationalist doctrine which we shall now consider.

The most serious charge which M. Maritain makes against existential philosophy, from his Thomistic point of view, is its "subjectivism." According to Thomism, the human person is not basically ordered to a world. "It is a substance equipped with properties . . . , a substance whose substantial form is a spiritual soul" (p. 81). Man is ontologically enclosed, existing, like a thing, within itself, and not stretched out originally towards other beings. I reach these other beings only through the operation of a special faculty, reason. But originally I am a thing, or substance, existing in myself and separated from them. Hence, since existential phi-

losophy is concerned with personal existence as it
is lived by the person from the inside, M. Maritain
accuses it of falling into an irresponsible egotism
which arbitrarily centers the world around a proud
and unreasoning self. "If I abandon myself to the
perspective of subjectivity, I absorb everything into
myself, and, sacrificing everything to my unique-
ness, I am riveted to the absolute of selfishness and
pride" (p. 75).

The intellect can grasp only objects which are
present before it: ". . . object and objectivity are the
very life and salvation of the intellect" (p. 13). M.
Maritain is prepared to admit that the objective
essences and natures, which are objectively known
in this way, do not exhaust the depths of our subjective existence. Something is omitted, but nothing
is deformed. ". . . In relation to its essential structures, the subject is in no wise betrayed when it is
made object. The objectisation [*sic*] which univer-
salizes it and sees intelligible natures in it, makes
it known by a knowledge destined doubtless to continue to deepen, but not one that is in any sense un-
just. Such objective knowledge does no violence to
the truth of the subject, but renders that truth
present to the mind" (pp. 80–81). My own existence, as I live it, is known only to God: "Only God
knows me in this wise . . ." (p. 77). Against St.
Augustine, M. Maritain asserts that man can have
no direct knowledge of his own existence from
within: "subjectivity is inconceptualizable; is an unknowable abyss" (p. 69).

Hence by abandoning the objectivity of reason
and by trying to penetrate into these forbidden
depths, existential thinkers, beginning with Kierke-

gaard, have fallen into a fantastic irrationalism which has "succeeded only in bringing about, in philosophy itself, a philosophical destruction of the intellect . . ." (p. 127). Having rejected essence and reason, nothing is now left for existentialism but the darkness of subjective existence: ". . . it sprang from a radically irrationalist thought which rejects and sacrifices essences, and falls back upon the night of subjectivity" (p. 131). An exclusive concern with the subjective and a rebellion against the light of reason are the two most basic charges M. Maritain brings against existential philosophy.

In addition to these, he makes two further criticisms of what he calls "the ethics" of existentialism. For M. Maritain freedom belongs to the faculty of will. There is no freedom of the intellect as such, for it is receptive and determined by its objects. But he speaks constantly of *freedom of the will,* and says that "the will begets the free decision in which ti *makes* its choice" (p. 91). The will, of course, should be guided by a consideration of rules based upon the essence of man and the fixed natures of things. But by disregarding all such formal structure and "by repudiating speculation in favor of action" (p. 47), "existentialism becomes voluntaristic" (*ibid.*), that is, it encourages a blind action with no concern for its natural end.

M. Maritain recognizes that existential thought has attempted to deepen and to radicalize the traditional conception of freedom as restricted to a mere freedom of the will. But for him "the whole root of liberty is established in the reason" (p. 82). According to him, "there are objective norms of morality, there are duties and rules" (p. 52), which we must

first consider and then follow exactly in our differ-
ing situations if we are to be free. Therefore "by
suppressing generality and universal law, you sup-
press liberty" (p. 60), and what remains, as the
moral teaching of existentialism, is "an absurd abyss
of pure and formless liberty" (p. 81).

These are the major charges brought by M. Maritain against the existential philosophy of our time.
Let us now examine them, not exclusively in relation
to the doctrines of Sartre, but also in relation to those
of Kierkegaard, Marcel, Jaspers, and, above all, to
those of Heidegger, so far the profoundest and most
disciplined existential thinker, about whom M.
Maritain has said very little. Do his charges hold
good against what we may call the central methods,
conclusions, and aspirations which these thinkers
share in common?

First of all, the authentic existential thinkers of
our time do not follow St. Thomas in accepting the
real distinction between essence and existence and
then in giving a certain priority to existence. What
is happening is rather that the whole distinction is
being questioned, with the result that a new way of
understanding existence is developing. For the tradition, as we have seen, essence is an invisible, determinate definition, or whatness, that is, taken
strictly, only a possibility for some cause or set of
causes. It gains existence when these causes bring
the essence out of themselves (*extra causes*) and
make it into a visible object present before the
senses and the mind. Heidegger and Sartre, among
others, have recognized that this picture of a definite
possibility becoming actualized in nature, while it
may apply to the building of a house from a blue-

print and to the manufacture of other artifacts, certainly does not apply to man. A human child does not start out with a definite picture of himself inscribed in his nature or in his mind. If he does accept such a picture which he then tries to realize, this comes from a choice made either by himself or by others who have persuaded him.

Furthermore, the act of existing cannot be reduced to an objective presence at a momentary now or at a succession of such nows. Human existence, as we live it, necessarily involves the future towards which I am moving and the past things and events through which I have passed. All the three phases of time—future, past, and present—are involved in this becoming which may gain or lose a peculiar unity or integrity of its own. The person is not automatically endowed with an essential unity from the very beginning, which merely has to be realized, like a blueprint. Human existence temporalizes itself, and its possible integrity faces many difficulties and dangers. It is won or lost by struggle and decision through time.

Traditional philosophy had a very inadequate and distorted notion of this temporal dimension of human history, which it broke down into a mere succession of present nows, as observed by a detached spectator. But the living of life cannot be observed from the outside in this way. It is active and concerned, ever ahead of itself as it moves toward the future. This becoming is pervaded by a radical freedom of awareness that can always gain a distance from any fixed frame of reference or system of essences. This does not mean, however, that human becoming exists in a totally disordered world with no intelligible structures of its own. But, as we shall see, these structures are not fixed properties, or forms, that can be abstracted from time. They are existentials, as Heidegger calls them, distinguishable ways of becoming through time. M. Maritain has not seen that it is the traditional concept of being as objective presence before the mind that is being questioned. The issue is far more basic than he believes.

His attack on existential thinking as a "subjectivist" philosophy also brings up a basic ontological issue. Is the human person a substance, or a thing, essentially determined and, therefore, enclosed within itself? Existential phenomenology has subjected this traditional conception to a very careful examination, and has found that it simply does not agree with the evidence. From its very beginning to its end, human existence is intentional or relational in character, stretched out spatially and temporally into a moving field of care. The carpenter is not substantially isolated from the house on which he is working. He is where his fingers are feeling the texture of the wood and in the whole life-space around him, which is not an abstract, geometric space, where he is laying the floor. Similarly the child is not subjectively isolated from its mother or its playmates.

The whole so-called problem of *other minds* is an artificial one which arises from an erroneous picture, derived from the Aristotelian category of substance and Descartes' exaggerated version of the mind as a thinking thing. The child's awareness is not enclosed within a separate mind. It inhabits the child's interests and activities, and, with them, it

reaches out to meet the responses and the sugges-
tions of its companions, as the awareness of a tennis
player must be already anticipating and preparing
for the next stroke of his opponent. If they are really
playing the game, they share a diffused double
awareness which is in the other as well as in the
self. When I am driving a car on a turnpike, I am
not simply located behind the wheel. Indeed, I had
better not be. I am behind the wheel only by being
ahead of myself and the car, 100 yards down the
road where I am going. I am where my attention is
riveted, where my care is taking me, in some region
of the human world. I am *in* this world not objectively, as a paper is in the drawer or as a drop of
water is in a glass. I am *in* this world as a field of
care, as we say that a young doctor is *in* medicine
or that a boy is *in* love.

I am not first locked up in a private subjectivity
from which I emerge by special processes of "knowledge" which take me out of myself. This subjectivist
picture, which M. Maritain shares with the central
tradition of Western thought, has led only to absurd
and unanswerable questions as to whether there is
any external world at all. The existential thinkers
have not merely rejected this false construction;
they have lucidly described many phases of our relational existence in the light of constraining evidence. They have shown that man is stretched out
into a world from which, as long as he exists, he
can never be separated. Theoretical knowing and
speaking presuppose this world. They are themselves special ways of being in the world.

This notion of the human life-world, *Lebenswelt*
as Husserl called it, is wholly absent from the major

traditions of Western philosophy. Not only is existential philosophy not subjectivist; it has now gone farther in working out a radically non-subjectivist view of human existence in the world than all those traditional forms of objectivism which have a kernel of subjectivism at their very root.

Recent phenomenological studies, beginning with those of Husserl, have shown that the world in which we live is centered around the moving body. M. Maritain calls this *egotism*. But this is to make a moral accusation against a fact. There can be little question that the oriented space in which I exist lies around my lived body and that its directions, forward and back, left and right, and up and down, are oriented with respect to the motions of this body. A careful analysis of ordinary language will make this clear. But it has nothing to do with egotism. This term may be properly applied to a version of the world that has become fixed and closed and which confuses itself with *the* world which encompasses and transcends it. But even a world version that is open to what it does not know and to what lies beyond it is still spatially and temporally centered in the lived body. If I am to order my existence to what transcends me, both I myself and the world in which I exist must be so ordered.

This self-transcendence can actually happen, though more rarely than we ordinarily suppose. As Kierkegaard showed with a remarkable lucidity, it is one thing to talk the language of transcendence; it is quite another to live and to exist in this way. When this does happen, I myself and my life-world are not eliminated. They are taken over intact, just as they are, and placed in a wider world of meaning. I could no longer exist in a world which completely failed to meet the needs of my lived body and which was, therefore, not in this sense centered in me. This is not egotism. It is a necessary condition of human existence, a basic fact of life.

M. Maritain claims that this world of our lived existence is an "unknowable abyss" and that the disciplined attempt to explore it by the so-called methods of phenomenology leads to a "destruction of the intellect." A region of existence is admitted to exist. But we are warned against exploring it because it is unknowable. In the past, when such warnings have been put forth by an established tradition, it has usually indicated serious limitations in this tradition and the need for a development of new methods and concepts. M. Maritain's statements are indications of this kind. Through the whole course of our Western history, what was called "immediate experience" has been disparaged and discounted as fleeting, chaotic, and most of all as *subjective*. In spite of what M. Maritain says, the subject is betrayed when it is approached as an object for, as Kant showed with unforgettable cogency, the subject simply is not an object. This does not mean, however, that there is no way of understanding it. New ways must be developed. And this is actually happening in our time.

Phenomenology is a new way of approaching this "subjective" existence as it is lived, which has already led to significant discoveries. One of the most important, as we have seen, is that this lived existence is not an isolated "subject" but a whole world horizon with structures and orders of its own. The traditional attempt to break it down into separate experiences, to insert them into a subjective container, then to disparage them as an "unknowable abyss," and finally to absorb them into an objective perspective is simply a strategic move in a great conflict that is opening up in our academic disciplines and in our culture. We may call this *a war of the worlds*. Which horizon is prior to the other? From which of the two is the other derived? Which is the wider and more inclusive—the objective universe of traditional reason and modern science or the life-world into which we are born, in which we pursue our chosen projects, and in which we face death?

By referring to this world horizon as "subjective" and "unknowable," and to our modern attempt to explore and understand it as an irrational "destruction of the intellect," M. Maritain shows clearly which side he has taken in this war of the worlds. For him, the perspective we achieve by regarding everything as an object out there from a detached point of view is the wider and prior horizon, from which the other is derived. The life-world may be placed in this frame as a flux of ineffable experiences contained within the isolated subject. These are really to be understood as objects, or things, among other things in a vast panorama of objects, located in an objective space, and succeeding one another in an objective time.

M. Maritain calls the opposing position irrational. If by *rational* we mean reason in the traditional sense, the examination and analysis of objects that can be brought before the mind and the senses, this is true. But if we mean, rather, discovering and bringing into the light the truth of things and existents, wherever and however they are, the disciplined exploration of the life-world, which has only recently begun, is an eminently rational enterprise. In any case, the war of the worlds that is now under way will not be decided by the mere use of invidious terms and epithets. It will be decided only by painstaking investigations of the evidence in relation to the question that must be constantly raised: which of the two horizons can encompass the other, in doing full justice to all the available facts, and with the least distortion and reduction?

Existential philosophy, in line with the evidence brought forth by recent clinical psychology, has raised serious questions concerning the traditional separation of human faculties and, in particular, concerning the traditional distinction between intellect and will. On this view, the intellect is strictly determined by its formal objects and is in no sense free. The will, on the other hand, has a limited freedom of choice between alternative means, each capable of getting us to the end. Existential thinking doubts whether any natural end has been inscribed on human nature and even whether the whole distinction between means and ends is applicable to our temporal existence as we live it. Can we divide this lived existence into definite periods having no value in themselves (means) and others in which we enjoy our rest (ends)? Is becoming ever finished? Does it ever achieve an end in which it can finally rest? In so far as it bears value, is it not the whole process, rather than this or that fragment, which is authentically human or unauthentic?

So far as the intellect is concerned, existential thinking is post-Kantian in its orientation. It can no longer hold that the human mind is wholly passive in merely receiving an external order that is already fixed and finished. New meanings, new ways of interpreting the world arise and pass away in history. When carefully read, the history of philosophy in the West is sufficient to show that the individual person has a certain freedom of mind which enables him to rebel against crystallized ideologies and to work out a way of life and understanding for himself, responsibly. This means that freedom is by no means restricted to a single faculty, the will, in making contingent choices between means for an end that is already fixed and established.

The whole world in which man exists, and over whose ordering he has some control, is constituted and pervaded with freedom. This does not mean, however, that existential philosophy is to be identified with an arbitrary and chaotic relativism. The existence into which we have been thrown has lasting limits, like chance, contingency, and death, and lasting conditions, like temporality, historicity, feeling, choice, freedom, and responsibility, which are always understood in a dim, pre-thematic way but which are always in need of further clarification, if authentic existence is to be achieved. It is true that existential thinking has found no evidence sufficient to support the claim that there are objective norms and principles valid for all mankind, irrespective of the different histories and circumstances of different groups. But this does not mean that it advocates "a pure and formless liberty."

"Value" is to be found in existing. Therefore we can say that any personal existence that evades or suppresses the lasting limits and conditions of this

existence is not truly human or authentic. Any existence, on the other hand, no matter to what particular
culture it may belong, if it meets these limits and
conditions, responsibly interprets them, takes them
over, and then lives them through to the very end
in a way that makes sense, is truly human and authentic. This must suffice as a brief indication of
the kind of answer that might be given, in a fuller
discussion, to the moral charges made by M. Maritain against existential philosophy.

This philosophy is neither essentialist nor existential in the traditional senses of these terms. It
is neither subjectivistic nor objectivistic in its point
of view, neither rational nor irrational. It defends
neither a voluntaristic doctrine of free will nor a
rationalistic theory of determinism. It is neither
relativistic nor absolutistic in its metaphysics. It is
a new way of thinking which has emerged in our
time and which has already shed a new light on
many lasting conditions and regions of the vast life-
world in which we actually exist. This world has
been long discounted and disparaged by traditional
philosophy, both ancient and modern. The new philosophy is still unfinished. But whatever else it may
turn out to be, it will be neither an authentic nor an
unauthentic form of Thomism. Its basic ontology,
its way of understanding, the kind of truth, and the
very world with which it is concerned are all very
different. We can fairly say that they are worlds
apart.

This is not to say that Thomism is not to be re-
spected as a great, creative expression of the human
spirit, relevant to its time, wide in scope, though

not sufficiently wide, and often penetrating in its insights.

These insights, however, have little or nothing to do with our lived existence and are exclusively concerned with the things one can see from a detached and objective point of view. We can learn much by following MM. Gilson and Maritain in their careful and illuminating studies of this great system. But we cannot learn by simply accepting it and by repeating its mistakes.

JOHN WILD

III / The Paradox
and Death of God
(KIERKEGAARD AND NIETZSCHE)

KIERKEGAARD AND NIETZSCHE? Certainly an even more dangerous comparison than usual. For in addition to the overriding difficulty of comparing any two thinkers, we are now to compare two individual human beings. They were least of all pure intellects addressing themselves to abstractly statable "problems" to which they found diverse "solutions," like arguing mathematicians. The thought of Kierkegaard and Nietzsche is inseparable from their inner lives and from the spiritual situation of their epoch. And it is not so much a "solution" to anything as a lived response to what they discerned as a crisis. What emerges then, as Karl Jaspers has insisted, is not a theory which can be "adopted," "agreed with," "refuted," but an elucidation of life to which each of *us* can respond.

If we say their work was a response to a spiritual crisis in the nineteenth century, we should also understand that this crisis was not something which the nineteenth century was itself consciously aware of; it took the genius of Kierkegaard and Nietzsche to sense that there was a crisis, and, in fact, both helped create the crisis by the very act of discerning it. What each in his own life and epoch discerned was that human life was on the point of losing all meaning to itself.

In the first half of the nineteenth century, Kierkegaard with superb wit and irony saw that now that the world had been baptized, become Christian, and lived and died within the horizon of the church, it had lost exactly what it thought it had found; the whole thing was a mockery of both Christianity and God Himself. It could not be that easy; and so Kierkegaard says that his mission is not to make things intelligible and easy again but to make them more difficult, as difficult as they really are. Precisely at the point where human life has found its meaning, understood it, ritualized it, institutionalized it, exported it to the benighted natives—that is the point where that very meaning has slipped away. "In an age where everyone is Christian, no one is Christian," Kierkegaard said. "There might be as many genuine Christians in an age as genuine poets—maybe one or two." Kierkegaard regarded his task chiefly as a "spy in the service of God": he would simply point out the perpetual discrepancy between word and deed, deed and proclaimed faith. All he wanted, he said, was *simple honesty;* lacking that, nothing made much difference. The profound and almost ineradicable inner hypocrisy which Kierkegaard detected has now become a technical term in professional existentialist thought: *Uneigentlichkeit, mauvaise foi,* inauthenticity. The inauthentic individual lies in a nether region between being and nonbeing; he is, and yet he isn't anybody, least of all himself. Does he genuinely exist? To be an honest individual is our first task for Kierkegaard, and eventually also our last.

In the second half of the nineteenth century, Nietzsche also discerned a comparable crisis: the century of *Kultur* was in fact nothing but a century of the herd, of the mediocre, of the inner slave full of self-loathing and resentment, of the "pale scholar," where no one had the health of spirit to affirm the meaning of his own life. Man had finally become a "sick animal," full of shame before others, remorse for his past, fear for his future, and always trembling before his self-created gods. He had found the sense of his life in obedience, in priding himself like a good servant on how well he performed tasks set by his masters; is this the meaning of life, asks Nietzsche, or is it not rather the symptom of a profound degeneration? Life can recover its own possible sense only if it can finally affirm itself; but this needs a type of man far harder, more courageous, and more vital than what has appeared so far.

Outwardly, neither of these partisans of life had much of it. No grand events. Kierkegaard passed as an esthete and dilettante in Copenhagen, a "writer." Later he was studied for his style in the schools. Nietzsche had a short university career in Basle as a professor of classical philology; he was finally driven by illness and restlessness to wander about alone in Switzerland and Italy, a mild-mannered

man with the somewhat weak eyes of a scholar.
Both were ill most of their lives, Kierkegaard with
a back injury, Nietzsche from an undiagnosed illness which may have been syphilis and which carried with it perpetual headaches, weaknesses, and
exhilarations. Kierkegaard collapsed physically and
died in 1855, from what he himself felt to be an
"excess of the spirit"; Nietzsche collapsed mentally
in 1889, passing from euphoria into mental blank-
ness, dying in 1900. The productive period of both
lasted something like ten years, during which they
wrote at an almost unprecedented pace. Their lives
were a merciless self-analysis and cultural diagnosis,
and both had a curious trajectory: rapidly increasing in radicalism and intensity, to a searing finale.
It is almost as if both had been maddened by what
they had seen: that what had passed as Christian
humanity was *not enough.*

There are similarities in the style of their thought;
and they are in fact among the very few thinkers
whose thought had a style. The whole gamut of expression is used: satire, irony, mockery, dialectical
argument, poetry, dialogue; and in the whole body
of their work, it is almost as if "reasons" were the
least important of their weapons. Whether it be
called literature or philosophy or something altogether new is hardly of much consequence. But it
is far more urgent, comprehensive, and dialectical
than what is usually taken as literature; far more
imaginative, passionately felt, and brilliantly styled
than what is usually taken as philosophy. It is not
merely the intellect to which they addressed themselves, but to the whole living man, which, of course,
also included his intellect. It is an expression de-

signed to effect a change in our sense of life and
not merely in our opinions. Readers therefore almost
from the start are instinctively attracted or repelled
by what is inherently upsetting; if they go straight
to the heart of the question, they cannot remain untouched. The question, as I have said, is the possible
sense of life; their diagnoses of the senseless are as
diverse as their responses.

Kierkegaard's response is dishearteningly simple:
God. But it is hardly in order to hear this word again
that we read him. What is unique in Kierkegaard
is the intensity and seriousness with which he develops the consequences. In a Christian society such
as that of Denmark in the first half of the nineteenth century, would not *everybody* have said the
same? Kierkegaard even thought from time to time
of entering the ministry. But he had another voca-
tion: irony. His doctoral dissertation was on the
subject, and it rather adequately defines his most
habitual mood: everybody believes in God, and yet
who does? Does anyone know what it would mean
to have faith in God? Kierkegaard was not a theologian and despised them; his task was theoretically
simpler and practically infinitely more difficult: to
attempt for himself to *exist* in the light of faith in
God, and to point out with a merciless wit the perpetual contradictions involved when a society with
its church and priests settles into the conviction that
it *is* Christian. Kierkegaard's pseudonymous writings, which evidently fooled very few, were largely
devoted to showing the dialectics of despair in life
and thought. His religious writings showed the religious consequences of belief.

For Kierkegaard, the supremely ironic display

was that of a Christian civilization or Christian Church. Is it possible for even a single man to be Christian? But that constitutes his *entire* task, and as Kierkegaard never tired of showing, each single man has exactly the same radical difficulties in becoming Christian that the first disciples had. Further, he will have the same difficulties tomorrow. These difficulties are not of a theoretical order; rather, they are existential. That is, the problem is not to *understand* Christianity but to become a Christian. For, among other reasons, Christianity cannot be understood or proven; if it could, it would be an affair for philosophy or science. It would rest on the successful result of reasoning or the experimental confirmation of a hypothesis; instead it openly declares itself to be a *faith*. This faith is interpreted by Kierkegaard not as belief in theories about Jesus but rather as a trust in God. The trust must be total, without reservation, unproven, and supreme in its claims. Against God, *nothing* else matters. And the nothing else is the world: father, mother, wife, children, reason, common sense, and oneself. Now such a faith can be *defined* in an instant, but that is not the problem; it is rather to live it. Only through an absolute faith in the absolute God can any individual escape despair. The individual who is not *constituted* by such a relationship to God *is* in despair. The thrashings about of the despondent soul appear in one form as a light-hearted estheticism, an uncommitted pursuit of pleasure and the "interesting." Don Juan is his classical name. Marriage is commital; Don Juan is a seducer. And Kierkegaard in *Stages on Life's Way* and *Either/Or* depicts the inner weather of such an existence with a wit, brilliance, and truth which could only be drawn from self-observation. The esthete is the wit *par excellence*. Everything is turned into wit, a shower of brilliant paradoxes which leaves the person of the speaker free and unassailable: he himself has said nothing. He *can* say nothing, according to Kierkegaard, since he *is* nothing but the self-conflicting display of masks.

The esthete is one fundamental possibility of human existence: the attitude that life is at bottom an entertainment which can be amusing or tedious but which is never to be taken at its serious face-value. The esthete is himself an entertainer who also wishes to be entertained; he exists in his purest form at the party, where nothing lasts too long, there is a good crowd of witty people each turning a different mask to each other, where no one talks excessively about anything and everyone finally finds his way home to an empty and exhausting rest. Kierkegaard notes in his diary: "I was the life of the party tonight; I came home and wanted to shoot myself." If life is a play and we the players, why indeed take any of it seriously? Does not human wisdom amount to esthetic detachment? And is it not folly to be too taken up with what is at bottom, nothing but a play of shadows? For Kierkegaard, the perpetual seduction of this attitude is the seduction of despair; and he found more than enough of it in himself.

Another "stage on life's way" is morality. If the esthete scintillates, saying something new on each occasion being bound by neither the rules of logical consistency nor the responsibilities of moral law, the moral man is "always the same." Don Juan is the classical esthete-seducer for Kierkegaard; he personifies morality in Judge William who, esthetically considered, is nothing but an intolerable bore. If the esthete always lives in the presence of others, "the crowd" as Kierkegaard defines them, the moral man on the contrary lives by and for moral duty, the impersonal, impartial moral law which remains the same from generation to generation, which is known by all men, and which commands unrelenting obedience. The moral man is a man inwardly committed and married to the eternal moral law: do good, shun evil. Responsibility and reliability are possible and demanded; promises are made and kept; regarding only the law and not persons, what the moral man tells one, he also tells the other; what he says yesterday, he will say tomorrow; if he, as judge, condemns his enemy, he will pronounce the same condemnation on his son or himself. The law is the same for all, impersonal, impartial, identical yesterday, today, and forever. The moral man is no entertainer but something far more serious, the responsibility on which a world can be built. He is not the seducer but the man of family. Kierkegaard's image of Judge William we can meet elsewhere in the busts of Roman senators: grave, strong, lined faces perhaps a trifle remote but with a remoteness which is that of a supreme law which cannot be flattered or bent to personal whim. In contrast the esthete looks like a bubble of iridescent gas.

But we are not at the end of "life's way"; in fact, we have not yet touched its supreme and most paradoxical form: the religious man. And here we can only *touch* it, Kierkegaard reiterates; it *essentially* evades communicability and rationality itself. The religious life is inherently absurd both to the esthetic and the moral lives; it is beyond both, living not in pleasure or in the natural reason of morality but in faith. Kierkegaard's early *Fear and Trembling* makes the contrast as directly as possible. Abraham was the "father of the faith"; in virtue of what? Abraham interpreted God's will as requiring the sacrifice of his son Isaac. Abraham, as we all know, then proceeded to carry out that will. That it was not finally consummated is nothing to the point; the point is that Abraham was *prepared* to sacrifice his only son. We must try to understand him at this moment. And Kierkegaard finds quite simply that it is *not* understandable; to kill one's son is neither esthetic entertainment nor moral conduct. What moral law could ever tolerate such an act? Could there be a moral law which would even *admit* the possibility of such a "sacrifice" of another without branding it as frankly the most hideous murder conceivable? Yet it was for precisely this faith that Abraham was called the father of the faith. What are we to make of it? Could any preacher advise the fathers in his flock to kill their sons whenever they heard such a thing from God? How did Abraham know it was God he heard and not the voice of Satan? It might even be more comprehensible if Abraham sacrificed himself, but it was his son; who is permitted to "sacrifice" another? Kierkegaard exhausts the possibilities of understanding the faith of Abraham, but it remains beyond comprehension. And yet that is what faith must be. To trust God is to abandon any ultimate trust in reason, common sense, prudence, moralities of principle, most of all, the detached excitements of the esthete. Faith to these other attitudes is pure madness; and yet, Kierkegaard urges, it is a madness which is the only sanity. For faith, every other form of human existence is despair. The faith in question is a *trust in God "for whom all things are possible"*; to take seriously such an Absolute Person is indeed to take lightly human reason and its morality. Faith "suspends the ethical," and with it, the impersonality and resignation implicit in any life inwardly determined by a "principle." God, Kierkegaard insists, is not a principle or law but an absolute person; the tensions of faith are those between a finite individual and an absolute individual; singularity and individuality are recovered only by suspending the ultimacy of universal laws and principles in order to trust in their source, God, who is not bound by these partial expressions of his will. But the "Knight of Faith" can at last dance. Outwardly he looks like everyone else, dressing, eating, doing his work like the rest of workaday mankind; inwardly he has at last found freedom, is rid of despair and resignation; but his freedom is incommunicable and beyond reason. He stands on his own feet, as himself, in an absolutely singular and unique relation to what is final, God as Person.

Faith of course is not a question of credal belief or of correct theology. Nor is it mystic union with God. It is more like the absolute trust a creature might have in his creator. It is not a career or profession and there are no "experts" in it; it remains a perpetual task and, Kierkegaard insists, our *only* task. "In life we have time for nothing else." Finally it is a relation between *individuals*. It is not made easier by the progress of mankind nor by science or political or religious reform. Only individuals can stand before God; they cannot sneak into an audi-

ence with him by being lost in the crowd of humanity. God therefore singles out the individual as an
individual; membership in a crowd is obliterated,
and that includes the crowd of Christendom. It is
only a decisive faith in God which enables an individual to *face* the crowd; unlike the esthete, his destiny does not lie before them. The individual can
become himself only before God; every other deter-
minant is but scattering and distraction. In that paradoxical faith, the individual can return to the world
and dance; it neither means everything to him, nor
is it opposed to moral law; everything can now find
its place. At least so Kierkegaard envisaged it in the
early *Fear and Trembling;* but it must be admitted
that this religious singing in the world found less
and less utterance in the course of Kierkegaard's
writing.

In any event, his diagnosis of himself and his
times found everyone wanting to be something more
or less than an individual. Men desired to become
Pure Reason, Science, Theology, Genius, leaders of
nations, even happy. Or they did not desire enough;
they were content to be a little of everything, to be
inconspicuous. But no one is inconspicuous to God,
and no one is called on to live in the "basement of
his own soul" reserving the parlor for guests. The
most difficult thing then is what to the world seems
either too easy or too presumptuous: to take oneself seriously as an individual, which means an individual before God. And that particular task is the
task of one's life, never finished, always in becoming, always in a paradoxical trust in what violates
one's own deepest common sense. If men have an
eternal destiny, which Kierkegaard never doubted,

then they have it as individuals who counted to God; there is an absolute meaning beyond current affairs, and any alternative in human existence is nothing but despondent evasion. However, above all, nothing in life can be seen, questioned, or changed, unless through that simple honesty which can call each thing by its straight name. Lacking that, nothing is possible. God has not departed from human society—he was never there in the first place. Kierkegaard finished his career with one of the most acidic attacks on the Church and Christendom which has ever been launched. He fully expected his house to be broken into by the mob, and to be stoned. Instead, the mob thoroughly enjoyed the fray, the newspaper in which it was published increased its circulation, and Kierkegaard became a kind of popular hero. After all, the mob had its *own* differences with the Church. Kierkegaard himself, the master ironist of spiritual life, observed everything. He died, never having "wanted to do anything but sit on a cloud all day long and sing hallelujah."

For Nietzsche, God is not paradoxical but dead. From the Greeks, we hear that all of Nature groaned when the great god Pan died. When Jesus died, the veil of the temple was rent. The death of *gods* is no slight matter; with Nietzsche it was excruciating and liberating. For the *first* time we have the opportunity to become ourselves, to become gods, mortal gods who "always look either straight ahead or down, never above." At last, Nietzsche dreamed, man need no longer be a slave or child of some "invisible" being, some eternal and perpetually frowning Person or Principle; we could be ourselves, and the final morality was no morality at all but "beyond good and evil," a pure rejoicing in life and the senses. Man, if he could only release himself from his ancient inner servitude to a higher principle or person, could at last be lord of his own life, exuberantly affirm it, divest himself of guilt and fear and finally live in a high noontide of affirmation which with Nietzsche bordered on a mystical experience of the present. In such a mood many times experienced, sometimes longed for, Nietzsche turned a remarkably perceptive eye upon what passed for culture, for morality, philosophy, for man. Man as he had hitherto defined himself was a disease, a degenerated animal. He had been too full of "self-loathing." Self-loathing gave birth to resentment of superiority in others, and all in all, what resulted was "morality," in which the superior and happy life were to be brought low in heaven and made to suffer for their joy. "The first shall be last" hope the slaves. Morality is experienced by the average man as some divine commandment or obligation, which would finally reward him in a world beyond for his obedient sufferings here. In point of fact, morality is nothing but the taste of the most vital, superior, and liberated men of the culture. Hence such a "free spirit" defines for himself and for others that which is good and bad, noble and ignoble; the rest following along take it as absolute and divine. The free spirit *creates* values; he does not take them over from society or from God, or from anywhere but his own free and vital tastes. Hence nothing could be worse for Nietzsche than the "pale criminal," who "once tasted the happiness of the knife" but now trembles before the judge. Let him affirm his own free and honest passions; he will find nothing better. At the same time, in place of moral rules, standards, "tables of value," we find Nietzsche extremely sensitive to *quality* of feeling, to *discriminations*, to *sensibility*. In place of a morality of rules, obligations, of the Thou Shalt Not, we find *taste*, the vital, lived taste of strong free men. Vulgarity, swinishness, brute force, simplicity of mind—none of these is anything but the style of the low. *High* and *low* in Nietzsche are decisive; they are the only differences among men, and they are definable only indirectly. No principles govern the judgment of *Übermensch*, and yet the man who could finally free himself from all nay-saying, from herd morality, superstition, other-worlds, from the inner dominance of the others, society and the mob, who could finally stand alone and free—such a man who can say at last *I am* is least of all an egotist for Nietzsche. He alone has genuine taste, self-discipline, discrimination, he is an *athlete* of the body and soul, perhaps a bit high-strung, but above all healthy, self-confident, and with a keen nose for the base, poisonous, and vulgar, for all those ideals and passions which lead to self-defeat and degeneration. In some moods, Nietzsche can even bring himself to think of Jesus as such an athlete of the spirit, clean, self-demanding, a touch of elegance, nothing of the loose and self-indulgent. His final apotheosis of man is man with full and exuberant health, aristocratic in spirit, who out of a richness of nature *can* be generous and appreciative of quality in others, who is not guilt-ridden, who does not fear death but is willing to "die at the right time." He despises, not from theory but instinct, all the noxious sentiments, ideas, and conformities of the "herd." By his own passionate being he *puts everything in its place,* establishes order, and keeps the whole mass of men from rotting in will-lessness, confusion, and fear Such is the *Ubermensch;* beyond man, beyond anything that has hitherto existed in any conspicuous fashion as "man." What is called for is fundamentally an aristocracy of the spirit and the body; Nietzsche never separates the two. Life is enough, Nietzsche seems to say, when it isn't ruined by fear, superstition, "self-loathing"; there is nothing *but* life, an infinitely complex and nuanced phenomenon. But back of it? Nothing.

The "metaphysics" of Nietzsche is interesting and in many ways remarkably contemporary, which is not necessarily a recommendation except for its accessibility to our own spirits. Being at bottom is pure chaos. There is no primordial order; there is nothing but chaos turning upon itself, looking nowhere, desiring nothing, throwing up in its random movements the most beautiful and fragile forms and without thinking twice engulfing them back into its own raging self. Being is in itself profoundly meaningless; to believe in a Providence, watching over the course of nature and bringing good out of evil, transforming disasters into heavenly or earthly triumphs, is nothing but the sheeplike dream of the timid who can't endure the hard facts. It is all senseless, and, further, as the ultimate facet of its senselessness, it is a *perpetually recurring* senselessness. Nietzsche regarded his doctrine of the "eternal return" as his "deepest" thought. He devised some proofs of no very great interest that everything must recur again and again, just as it is, and, furthermore, has already recurred an infinite number of times. Our interest here is not with the adequacy of his proofs but with the meaning of this idea to him: if indeed everything we are, do, struggle for, hope for, live for, has already been done and must be done and redone an infinite number of times, then what do we behold? The image of perfect futility. Now, reasons Nietzsche, if this is the ultimate meaninglessness of life, what can the free spirit make of such a vision? It becomes in his hands the *test* of ultimate strength and absolute affirmation. If you can still affirm your life in spite of this monstrous truth, if you can honestly say: let the wheel have another turn, then indeed you have conquered all despair. You have, in fact, affirmed with full heart the overarching senselessness of all existence. At this point, everything begins to *sing*. There are no more defeats for the spirit, since it affirms itself above the chaos and senselessness. What can it fear now that it affirms meaninglessness itself?

The other aspect of this vision is that to *become* chaos is the sure mark of the sickening man. Vitality —strength, self-affirmation, health of body and spirit —is inherently an *imposition of an order*. Each vital center to live must not so much "adapt itself to the environment" as adapt that environment to itself, create the circumstances in which it can live; force therefore is the necessary corollary of living itself. Nothing could be more foreign to Nietzsche's heart than *deference*. To live essentially is to *impose* order, not to accept it from another. It is to master the chaos. Furthermore this mastery of the other is the destiny and good of the other. The sun, he says, does not ask permission to shine; its being *is* shining, and with his shining, all weaker stars are blotted out. So be it. Weaker hearts cannot stand the slaughter, but then they condemn themselves to die. Only strength, vital affirmation, *mastery* lives. Obviously all this is profoundly anti-Christian. What of mercy, charity? What of the Sermon on the Mount? All, according to Nietzsche, are deeply *anti-vital*. The Christian religion is therefore the sentiment of the defeated, not the masters; take your choice: sicken with Christian sentiments or live the new with Zarathustra. Christianity is nothing but an enormous self-loathing on the part of humanity; let there be a new man who can affirm himself. Affirmation of life, moreover, is the only source of even the finer Christian virtues, such as charity, generosity, love. Only the superabundant have anything to give.

The "free spirit," needless to say, has not freed itself from life but for it. Fettering its freedom is remorse for all it did which it should not have done. And so its first hard task: to affirm the past, all that past, just as it was. Or it may be fettered by fear and concern for the future, for its own death. But let it finally accept death, for the wheel of existence turns and turns and all things recur. Or it dreads the judgment of others, the mob; for this it need only cultivate the "Great Contempt." Or it stands in awe before God; for this it needs an inextinguishable laughter. All the gods tremble before laughter; and the best of them laugh at themselves. Even "nature" and "fact" or general objective "truths" are no final impediments to absolute freedom. For Nietzsche, we must learn to understand truth or what we take to be final facts as "interpretations" of a hidden text. Our truths at bottom are what serve our own life; all "ideas," "propositions," "perceptions" are nothing but perspectives on a chaos, dictated by the vital interests of the organism having them. There is no *possibility* of the mind mirroring an independent nature, nor would there be any *purpose* in the redu-plication. To think, to affirm as true—are all just so many ways of interpreting, forming, molding the flux of chaotic experience, selecting out of it what is useful to life; fact is not a block to the free spirit, it is its own work. All ideas are oversimplifications and "lies"; truth itself Nietzsche defines as a "vital lie."

So liberated, the free spirit can at last live in the present, experience its own exuberant life as all there is and more than enough. If the spirit could finally seat itself where it is, affirm its own life as it is, it would live in the Great Noontide. Surrounded by the blue dome of heaven, it could at last sing and dance and live in a "joy far deeper than sor-row," a joy which "wants everlastingness." Only such a spirit is the justification for the sufferings and weepings of mankind. It is at last the "meaning of the earth." It justifies itself by saying "I am." It has transcended by absorbing and conquering all the negative, chaotic, nay-saying poisons in life and has transformed them into joy. The elevation and quality of spirit is measured by that which it has overcome. The elevation Nietzsche envisaged had overcome the distinction of good and evil, overcome chaos, overcome the senselessness of eternal recurrence, overcome all its own tendencies toward decline, sor-row, remorse, fear, awe, finally to be able to affirm in full heart the whole joyous risk of life itself. Nietzsche's own conscious career terminated with what seemed to be a manic exuberance followed by what to all human communication looked like an inner night.

The polarity of these passionate thinkers is instructive. To read them with the slightest sympathy is to feel at once the flatness, confusion, and distraction of one's own existence. In comparison, virtually every other thinker seems sold-out to something less than the absolute. The existential exhilaration of these two however, authentic as it was in themselves, presents a temptation of radical *ambiguity*. Neither in the least wanted disciples; and yet both are evidently urging a form of existence upon us with almost unrelenting seriousness and power. How then are we to respond? Each, of course, for himself. The response which neither would have cared for and which would be incompatible with their thought would be to accept a "little" of their radicalism but only "to a degree." The *essence* of what they urged admitted no degrees. What would any such assimilation mean except a flat contradiction of what they urged? *Nothing but God,* says Kierkegaard, and we add, trying our best to assimilate him, except a *bit* of the world. *Affirm life,* says Nietzsche; we add, except when it is cruel, violent, and immoral. Our exceptions cancel the idea. But, while it would be impertinent here to wish to suggest improvements upon the thinking lives of these heroes of the spirit, it may not be impertinent to suggest that while both articulated decisive modes of authentic human life, human life may not be *exhausted* by these alternatives. There are other modes which are authentic, which see in existence other factors not so visible in the radicalisms of either Kierkegaard or Nietzsche. And while these may appear as "weaker," they are so only to the implicit radicalisms in ourselves; in their own right, they may define a different strength. For ultimately what impresses nearly every reader of Kierkegaard or Nietzsche is a troubling *impatience* in their spirit. Let us look again at their self-imposed task: to see to the bottom of life, to diagnose the culture of their times, to see clear through themselves, and on the basis of this comprehension to propose directly or indirectly radical alternatives to what they saw. But it is far from being certain that either one man's life or the life and culture of an epoch can surrender its final meaning in this *or any other way*. Both Kierkegaard and Nietzsche arrived at certitudes about life: one that its sense was only its sense before a transcendent God, the other that its sense was only its sense to its own self-affirmation. And so has each finally grasped it? But their comprehensions were as different as the individual Kierkegaard was from the individual Nietzsche. "Agreement" here could be nothing but coincidental and illusory; it is not a clear and univocal proposition which is proposed to us but rather two lives. The astonishing thing about both lives is their passion to get to the bottom of life, to see through it and settle its sense once and for all. Most men have either more indifference or more humility toward such a theme. Kierkegaard and Nietzsche rightly reprove our indifference; but, I believe, they also offend our humility. The humility they offend is, needless to say, not a subservience to other men, their words and their deeds; but at best it might be a spiritual humility which stands a little more in awe before the phenomena and tasks of life itself. Is indeed life—not everyone's life, or the life of others, but my own life—the *sort* of thing which I can see through right now, grasp, and *on the basis of that grasp* reform from the ground up? The radicalisms of both Kierkegaard and Nietzsche spring from an impatience toward a mystery. If our own lives are the sorts of things *about* which we can talk but which are not exhausted in that talk, then perhaps the appropriate attitude towards our own and others' lives is more like *listening* than ordering. As we listen to our own lives, the listening itself may quietly and indirectly alter its quality and direction. It is far from certain that the role of reflective spirit is to seize the reins of life and reverse its direction; nor is it passively to watch. But are these our exclusive alternatives? In a word, are there not an infinity of possible authentic human lives, as many as there men, as well as an infinity of possible inauthentic lives; and before such a problem, perhaps it is not exactly appropriate for the spirit to occupy the judge's seat even toward itself. Judgment and ordering without listening to what is being judged and ordered are *ipso facto* inappropriate. Yet if we begin to listen in humility to the depths of life, are we not in danger of capsizing? Of succumbing to the great "what is"? Neither Kierkegaard nor Nietzsche were in that danger; but there is more than a suspicion of their impatience with the genuine depths of their problem.

In any event, very few men have achieved anything like the perceptiveness of these spirits, the lucidity of self-observation, or the concern with the seriousness of the problem. Even if they do not speak for all of us, they speak for enough in any man to raise problems such as very few other philosophers have dared. Neither wanted disciples; but both deserve our most profound response.

WILLIAM EARLE

IV / Man as the
Impossibility of God
(SARTRE)

The major philosophical work of Jean-Paul Sartre is *Being and Nothingness*,[1] subtitled *an essay in phenomenological ontology*. It appeared in 1943, a work of 722 pages. In 1953 another extraordinary work appeared, *Saint Genet, Comedian and Martyr*,[2] a book of 573 pages serving as an introduction to the collected works of Jean Genet. In 1960 Volume I of a new work, *Critique of Dialectical Reason*,[3] made its appearance, a work of 755 pages. All of this in addition to four novels, some five short stories, nine

[1] *L'Etre et le Néant* (Paris, 1943); translated by Hazel E. Barnes, *Being and Nothingness* (New York, 1956).

[2] *Saint Genet* (Paris, 1952).

[3] *Critique de la Raison Dialectique* (Paris, 1960).

plays, three volumes of literary essays, a work on Baudelaire, and almost countless essays and shorter books on philosophical and political subjects. But the first three mentioned books give clearly enough an outline of the horizon of his philosophical thought. If *Being and Nothingness* develops the fundamental principles of Sartre's philosophy of freedom, *Saint Genet* analyses the person and works of the writer as illuminated by those fundamental principles; the *Critique of Dialectical Reason* extends the analysis to the social group and to history.

The style of Sartre's thought is clearly exhibited in *Being and Nothingness*, an incredible alternation between analyses of extreme abstraction and examples of those abstractions given dramatically. The initial impression is that of incongruity, of a *tour de force;* a closer reading removes some of this impression but never all of it. There remains something of the preposterous in Sartre's project of comprehending the individuality and lives of men through the exclusive aid of categories as poverty-stricken as his favorites, Being and Nothingness. What is equally fascinating however is how successful he sometimes is. At one moment we try to follow a delicately balanced analysis of the dialectical relations between being-in-itself and being-for-itself; the next our attention is turned to fakes, frauds, hypocrites, or to the embarrassment of others staring at us, the human body, its sexuality, love, hate, sadism, masochism, etc. And unquestionably we see something in these phenomena we never saw before or perhaps never saw in quite this way. For the most part, philosophical literature has chosen not to look at the underside of life at all, which is the side which most attracts Sartre. The noble, heroic, or saintly are phenomena which particularly arouse his ire, and he never tires of lambasting the bourgeoisie. They are one and all walking self-deceptions, examples of Nothingness falsely solidified into Being, which he has already demonstrated to be an impossibility. Animating his work is a love for freedom, a nausea for pomposity, smugness, and the "decent," and the spirit of nose-tweaking which Simone de Beauvoir records as characteristic of Sartre as a young man. Fundamentally a philosopher, Sartre is not content to scoff at the establishment and its servants; he must also *demonstrate* their nullity. And the truth is that he goes a long way toward succeeding. Nevertheless Being and Nothingness in their stark opposition are not necessarily the most appropriate or commensurate categories for illuminating concrete human life; and too frequently in Sartre's pages we have the impression of having stumbled into a room of some dingy left-bank hotel, where we can see only by the light of a single bulb hanging from the ceiling. It casts sharp shadows and throws a glaring light but our friends are hardly recognizable. And undoubtedly such artificial illumination shows us something—we shall try here to suggest what—but equally certain it is that we are under no compulsion of logic or ontology to see only by the light Sartre's categories provide.

Since Sartre's analysis of human behavior rests upon his "phenomenological ontology," we had best begin with that. *What appears* to us will be our ultimate foundation of evidence and not what we merely infer or believe to be. And appearance in its most general sense is always of a *being* or object of some sort, but also it is an *appearance of* that being. In a word, the whole phenomenon as a phenomenon is analyzable into two fundamental terms: a being, and an appearance of that being. Or, in looser language, any consciousness is the consciousness of some object; the object is what it is, a being; our consciousness of that object is what *it* is, consciousness. But now: is our consciousness itself simply another kind of *being,* another form of object? Clearly not; for if the act of consciousness were an object, and the object of which it was conscious, another, then we should merely have two objects without one being *conscious* of the other. Hence our acts of consciousness as we subjectively perform them are not related to their objects as one being to another; rather, to be conscious of anything is precisely *not* to be it, and to be conscious of being is to not-be being. The not which is here in question is an *internal* negation of being. Consciousness then is being internally negating itself. External negation holds between objects insofar as some consciousness distinguishes them; the inkwell is externally *not* the pen, but the "not" here is only in a third something, in the mind which distinguishes them. It makes no internal difference to either inkwell or pen. But consciousness is the *internal* nothingness of its object. The consciousness of any being is the not-being of that object such that the pair consciousness-object constitutes an internal negation. Thus Sartre arrives at his chief contention, that consciousness is a pure internal negation, a lived contradiction. "It is what it is not; and it is not what it is," Sartre says. But that which is self-contradictory cannot *be,* we say at once. Precisely, answers Sartre; consciousness *is* this nothingness. Human being is that being through which Nothingness comes into the world.

Consciousness is always directed to some being, that being of which it is the internal negation; but it is also implicitly or "laterally" aware of itself. In short, to be conscious is to be in some way conscious of one's consciousness without one's own consciousness being the direct theme of attention. Consciousness, thus, is *for itself* but *of* another being which it is not. And so we arrive at the two chief terms of Sartre's analysis: Being is being-in-itself; Nothingness appears as being-for-itself. Nothingness (or consciousness) is adjectival to Being, since it is only the negation of it; without Being-in-itself no consciousness would exist. Consciousness is a "decompression" in the "solidity" of Being, a "hole," a "perpetual flight" not merely from Being but also from itself. It is a "wind" constantly blowing outward towards the world. Consciousness not merely is the nothingness of being, it is also the nothingness of itself; for if it should ever relapse into being something, it would by that very fact no longer be conscious. Hence it is a double nothingness, both of being-in-itself or its direct object, and also of *itself*; it is pure and perpetual self-annihilation.

If consciousness as such is its own nothingness, any form of it will disclose the same nothingness: knowing, perceiving, dreaming, imagining, feeling, desiring, etc. are all modes of "nihilating" the world and self; and Sartre devotes separate analyses to all of these. To desire an object is not-to-be-that-object, in such a fashion that not-being-it constitutes the very essence of the desire. Desire is thus a lack of

being; and once again we see a display of the ontological category of nothingness. Consciousness is
perpetually a "lack of being," and in this very not-
being lies its *freedom from* being. It never "coincides
with itself," is always "thrown out into the world,"
is nothing but a project into a future which it has
not caught up with. In many metaphors, Sartre reiterates his contention that consciousness is a living
self-contradiction, "condemned" to free existence because it cannot *be*. The very temporality inherent
in our existence is reducible to the internal explosion
which consciousness is.

If this is being-for-itself or consciousness, what
can be said about being-*in*-itself? We must understand
that being-in-itself is being defined as abstracted
from all its relations; external relations among
beings exist only for a witnessing consciousness
which relates them; internal negations are consciousness itself. If then a being is abstracted from all its
relations, indeed nothing is left with which to char-
acterize it. Being-in-itself is "absurd," just and only
itself, pure identity. It is through the introduction
of consciousness or Nothingness that all the indi-
viduations, relations, and possible characterizations
of an object come into appearance. Temporality,
spatiality, possibility, number, etc. are all so many
forms of intelligibility brought by consciousness to
being; one and all, they reveal by analysis that they
derive from that primordial nothingness which is
consciousness. If *per impossibile* we abstract Nothingness or consciousness from the apparent world,
there remains only the inert, solid, dark, ineffable,
and even "nauseating" plenitude of unilluminated
being-in-itself. The nothingness of consciousness,

then, is the very light by which anything appears to us, a light moreover which is itself responsible for the structure (though not the being) of what it shows.

But although knowledge supplies us with a guiding thread for the analysis of the nature of being-in-itself and consciousness, we should not suppose that it is the basic form of the relation of consciousness to being; *that* form Sartre designates as the *project*. Consciousness or conscious man or man simply is fundamentally *projective,* and this again conforms to Sartre's basic notion of self-contradiction. If man is inherently the very embodiment of self-contradiction, he is restless in essence, existing always towards a future possible which he is now not. He inherently lacks being; and if he were ever to simply be and not be *towards* something he is not, he would no longer be conscious. As consciousness, what he lacks is exactly that being he projects; and his most fundamental project is finally to become something, to *be* at last. This is a satisfaction inherently denied him except of course in death. If consciousness is a "hole" in being, then it is a hole whose sole project is to be filled up. But it must be filled in a certain way; not simply filled, which would be extinction, a relapse back into the unconscious being-in-itself of objects, but to be *at once* filled and empty, in order to be *conscious* of being filled. Sartre sees at the end of every human project this paradoxical aim, both to-be and not-to-be in one and the same act, to *be* happy or satisfied, to both desire and to have the object of one's desire, in general to actualize value. Such a fulfillment man dreams of as God; an eternally blessed being who *is* eternally, yet is in the form of being *conscious* of it, hence *not* being it at all! But this aim is clearly a contradiction in terms. Consciousness is inherently finite and inherently not-being; bliss could be eternal only at the cost of losing consciousness of it. Hence man is pure restlessness, pure project, pure longing for what he can never be; as Sartre finally puts it, "Man is a futile passion." The light of consciousness longs to extinguish itself in darkness; but it must also enjoy its own extinction, *see* it.

However, what at first glance looks like not merely a human but a cosmic disaster has another side. If the synthesis of for-itself and in-itself, or consciousness and being-in-itself is impossible, hence if *God* is impossible, and there is no ontological foundation in the cosmos for an ultimate meaning, intelligibility, or value towards which we might strive and against which we might measure our opinions, then man is absolutely free at last. If, as Nietzsche said, God is dead, then this death constitutes the liberation of man. There now is nothing but individual human projects, human freedoms, human consciousnesses, and no objective cosmic standards against which they may be measured. We now have the clear theoretical justification for the finality of the *human;* and Sartre at times is perfectly willing to call his existentialism a "humanism." The scene has been cleared of any natural or theological aims or values; we do not have some nature according to which we must live; for there is no essence of freedom or nothingness, there are no standards of value independent of our own free affirmations. In a word, man now has theoretical permission to do what he must in any case do: make his own life. Man has no essence or nature, since any such idea would freeze his inherent freedom into an "object," endow it with being-in-itself. His free existence always precedes his essence; or put otherwise, his essence is merely the record of what he has done, a backward glance on his past accomplishment. His freedom however is precisely a freeing of itself *from* that dead past and *for* a future projected from a present situation which takes on its particular outlines from that project. Freed thus from any values-in-themselves, truths-in-themselves, or closed situations-in-themselves, all of these now being dependent upon the free project of consciousness, Sartre discovers an exhilaration of freedom comparable to Nietzsche's. Man can come into his own now that he has seen through the gods. Neither Sartre nor Nietzsche, of course, regards such a situation where *everything* hangs upon man's own freedom as an invitation to frivolity. Freedom is only authentic when the exhilaration is deepened with anxiety, despair, and a sense of abandonment. If everything hangs upon my own freedom, then indeed I *may* do whatever I like, but had I not better take care what I choose to do and, indeed, what I like?

But at this juncture we find ourselves in the terrain usually assigned to ethics; and Sartre's ethics centers on the concept of *authenticity*. If man cannot solidify his restlessness into *being* anything, he can at least exist authentically in his own form of not-being, of freedom; then at least he will not be deluded by vain supports. In a few places in *Being and Nothingness* Sartre alludes to a form of consciousness which is not a futile passion, which is not perpetually self-deceived but which is lucidity itself. It would seem that by grasping and affirming the truth of my own free nothingness, I can at least escape a certain bad faith or hypocrisy which otherwise might be a permanent temptation. To exist in freedom is anxiety; my freedom has no supports, no doctrines, authorities, customs, revelations, or proofs to consult for decision. The entire sense I make of my life and of that of others as well as the world is not a given datum which I read on the surface of things but is something made by me, and made in freedom. In a word, all sense is up to me. True, I find a certain "coefficient of adversity" in my situation in the world. I cannot *in fact* do everything, be everywhere, or have any particular past I like; but I still retain my absolute freedom of making *sense* of these limits, in choosing what attitude I shall take toward them, in choosing what I shall do with my situation. Even death, while an inevitable fact, nevertheless becomes a meaningful fact only insofar as *I* give it some sense: regret it, ignore it, or orient my life in its light. My complete *responsibility* for every existential meaning is a responsibility which I cannot avoid, since even if I accept an interpretation or an evaluation from others, it is still I who must freely accept it. The implicit consciousness of my responsibility thus is an *anguished* freedom. "Man is condemned to be free," responsible alone for what he makes of himself, for how he values or interprets his life. No wonder then that consciousness is perpetually seduced into rejecting its responsibility, into making excuses for itself, into dodging its role of total responsibility and understanding itself in terms which mask the facts. This self-excusing mood, called "bad faith" by Sartre, is our *normal* consciousness. It is the sense of things adopted by the religious consciousness where, instead of taking personal responsibility for its values, it interprets them as established already by the revelation of God's will, by authority, by tradition. Or it is the consciousness of those who plead that they "can't help it," they are "made that way." Fortune failed to smile at their birth, they live in unpropitious times, had bad parents, bad heredity, or are afflicted with neurosis as though even that were not their own freely chosen response to their situation. Sartre sees these as so many forms of determinism, in which consciousness deliberately deceives itself into believing it is an object of some sort at the mercy of forces external to it. But how could the pure nothingness of consciousness be subject to external objective forces, to a causality of being? For itself, consciousness is never anything but a purely spontaneous, free source of meanings and projects; it is without excuse, and every form of determinism is merely a project of bad faith by which the anxiety-ridden consciousness takes refuge in objective facts, in natural laws, in exactly that which it is not and cannot be.

The alternative to such a bad faith is that lucidity which affirms its own pure nothingness, pure freedom, and pure responsibility in anguish. It is a consciousness without defenses which "exists" its freedom instead of refusing it. If we are pure freedom, then even our inner denial of it, bad faith, is itself a manifestation of freedom. We are wholly responsible for making these systematic excuses to ourselves and for ourselves; we are responsible for our neuroses, our sloth, for the deception by which we almost succeed in masking our own freedom from ourselves. To exist inauthentically, then, is to live as though we were not free and provided with a supply of excuses for every occasion. To exist authentically is to act in the full lucidity of one's total responsibility and, further, of the overarching futility of the human project as such.   */ 0 0 2 / 8*

If these reflections appear so abstract as to be useless for the comprehension of human existence, Sartre partially demonstrates otherwise in at least two existential analyses, that of Baudelaire and the extensive study of Jean Genet. There is no question in either of causally explaining a life. Sartre rather endeavors to insert his own sympathetic consciousness into the life, aided by a thorough knowledge of both the works and the circumstances of the life, in order to plumb the essential project of the man, to disinter those radical decisions and responses which created both the life and works. The decisions themselves are not explained; they belong to the realm of freedom. It is in *their* light that the various acts and expressions of the life are to be understood. *Saint Genet* in particular forms an essential counterpart to *Being and Nothingness;* it reveals both the fruitfulness of Sartre's existential analysis and also its limitations. The analysis, unlike the Freudian, seeks to disclose the most fundamental choices which the subjects made in their freedom, in giving sense to existence—how, in other words, they created themselves. And since these choices were choices of how to exist, they eventually involved the deepest ontological levels. To discover the *fundamental* project is Sartre's intention, and the foundations are always ontological: how to exist. From a clarification of the basic project, Sartre tries to show the appropriateness of the writer's choice of theme, his style, his favorite imagery, the mood and morale of his writings. In all these analyses, the incidents in the man's life, writings, attitudes toward politics, etc. are understood when seen to be consequent upon the project which is the man. There is no question of generalizing from a heap of details; rather, the effort is to penetrate through to that basic project which serves like a principle or rule to generate the particular manifestations.

There can, of course, be no *method* which could guarantee the success or sensitivity of its own application; and while Sartre's efforts to comprehend writers like Baudelaire and Genet inevitably betray the interests and preoccupations of Sartre, they still remain remarkably provocative studies. According to rumor, Genet himself after spending an afternoon in Sartre's apartment reading here and there in *Saint Genet* is supposed to have tossed it back on the table and remarked: "Ça va."

Sartre devotes a chapter to saintliness in order to justify his judgment that Genet pursues sainthood through abasement.[4] The saint, for Sartre, however, is not altogether one of the modes of human authenticity; the title of his book therefore is derisory. Socially considered, the saint is nothing but a phenomenon of societies devoted to consumption. "The saint is a de luxe flower which grows in the warmth of a single sun: the money of the Church." Voluntary impoverishment Sartre regards as the medieval version of a potlatch; an aristocrat by giving away his goods or giving them to the Church for decoration exhibits his superiority to the common poor,

[4] *Saint Genet,* pp. 76 ff.

who, having nothing to give and living closer to the necessities of life, are thereby abased. If a society exists for the sake of consumption, it realizes its end in the consuming destruction of its economic products; and to destroy them *for nothing* is the supreme mark of excellence. But to give away all one's goods is only to reaffirm the absolute right of ownership. The wealth is made by the workers from whom it is taken by the idle for a ritual destruction of which no one enjoys the benefit.

Western society today in contrast to the "democracies of the East" is ambiguous, being only partly a society of production and partly that of consumption. Everything is mixed up, and Sartre avows his desire "to help abbreviate the convulsions of the dying society, aid in the birth of a community of production, and to help raise with the workers and the militant a new table of values." This is why saintliness is repugnant to me, with its sophisms, its rhetoric and morose delectations; it has only one use today, to allow men of bad faith to reason badly." The feudal society in which saintliness flourished Sartre sees as dominated by a black aristocracy, full of parasitism, violence, potlatches, indolence, a taste for death, and ostentatious destruction. It is not the society of production.

"Christianity, great syncretic movement, has accommodated other moralities. Religion of the state, it prescribed to the middle-class citizens economy, temperance, and a sound management of their fortune. Religion of class, it preached resignation to the lower classes. It spoke everybody's language. It urged that there was only one Christian morality, the same for all; its priests were clever enough to make the poor believe that their resignation before the riches of other was, at bottom, of the same essence as the joyous renunciation of the aristocrat. In both cases, it was said, one turned from the goods of the earth. . . ."

"In this sense, the saint in an aristocratic society has the function of mystification: his destitution is presented as an example to the poor and falsely identified with theirs" (*Saint Genet,* p. 188). Socially, therefore, Sartre's views of Christianity merely repeat those of Marx. In a word, religion is seen as the opium of the people.

Inwardly, saintliness is the same consumption, but now of oneself; one destroys oneself, becomes a nothing in order to offer this precious gift to God. But Sartre is quick to perceive the secret pleasure of the saint in being nothing, or his exquisite sorrow which amounts to the same thing. No, says Sartre, "I do not present these contradictions in order to condemn Christian morality: I am too convinced that *every morality* is at the same time impossible and necessary. I describe." And in the case of Jean Genet, he is "living the impossibility of living." But then it isn't long before this is forgotten, and we find Sartre "denying saintliness wherever it manifests itself, among the canonized as well as in Genet." Sartre's nose is particularly offended by its "secularized disguises" in Bataille, Gide, and Jouhandeau. "It is always, in my eyes, nothing but the mystic branch of the generosity of consumption."

What repels Sartre most, not merely here in his analysis of the life of Genet but virtually everywhere, including his most abstract works, seems to be any value which is only for the singular consciousness itself, the private, that which is only in the interority of the mind or vis-à-vis God. His early short work *The Transcendence of the Ego* attempted to demonstrate that there was no ego primordially in consciousness; my ego is but a *construction* of my consciousness and is no more accessible to me than to others examining me.[5] And with this, he rejoices that now man is "plunged back into the world," "there is no longer anything of the *subject*." There is no transcendental ego, which would "pull a part of man out of the world"; "the me" now is revealed as endangered before the world and therefore drawing the whole of its contents from the world. "No more is needed in the way of a philosophical foundation for an ethics and a politics which are absolutely positive." And so it is the private interiority of consciousness that Sartre loathes; hence, to revert to his judgments-not-judged, Sartre finds that Genet's inner travails "remain without any deep efficacity." The movements of his soul remain symbolic, rhetorical; he mimes suffering, suffering yet not suffering. The whole drama takes place as if in a monk's cell: mere "states of mind; meanwhile the world follows its own course." And in *Critique of Dialectical Reason,* Karl Jaspers is excoriated for "refusing to cooperate *as an individual* with the history which the Marxists are making."[6] Sartre sees him as "fleeing the real movement of action into an abstract subjectivity whose unique end is to attain a certain intimate

[5] *The Transcendence of the Ego,* trans. Forrest Williams and Robert Kirkpatrick, New York, 1957). The original French version appeared in *Recherches Philosophiques,* VI (1936–37).

[6] *Critique de la Raison Dialectique,* p. 22.

quality." Our concern here is not with the merits of
this interpretation so much as with what it reveals
of Sartre: the value of the real, of efficacity, of action; and on the other hand the self-deception and
bad faith of the "mere" self, its intimate life, its
singularity, its transcendental aspirations, in short
the "religious."

The Genet book is astonishing. Sartre is obviously fascinated with his subject, although evidently
in interviews with Genet the fascination was not
reciprocated; but, and Sartre himself reports all this,
it is part of Sartre's merit to be fascinated with the
lives of men whereas Genet's indifference to Sartre
is only further manifestation of his closed spirit.
Sartre assures the reader in a number of places that
he is disgusted with Genet but no more so than he
is with many other phenomena. Sartre holds his nose
as he dwells on Genet's homosexuality and affirms
in a number of places that he himself has no such
loves. But he does not, to my recollection, equally defend himself against being a thief. He even half
satirically offers a prayer that Genet be treated well
by his readers, but it is not certain exactly what this
means except perhaps that they duplicate Sartre's
own ambiguous emotion of attraction-repulsion toward the "Saint." There are very few writers who
expend such a fascinated attention upon what they
explicitly judge to be hideous, bankrupt, old-fash-
ioned, and profoundly evil.

And most of Sartre's plays dramatize the fundamental situation of men coming to realize or avoiding a realization of their own free responsibility and
the human situation in which they must act. In *The
Flies*, Orestes finally affirms his own freedom, acts

in defiance of Zeus, at which point Zeus fades away as an impotent phantom whose only power was given to him by the belief of men. There are no forces which can compel the freedom of consciousness; whatever seems to possess overwhelming power owes it solely to a refusal of freedom to challenge it. Elsewhere Sartre says that even if God did exist, everything would remain unchanged; we would remain exactly where he says we are, solely responsible for our own free affirmation or denial, our acceptance or rejection of his supposed will. Sartre at his earliest was a Prometheus bringing absolute freedom to man; as he ages, we detect a certain recalcitrance in accepting all its expressions. Orestes is beautiful. But Genet? Baudelaire? Gide? Or the "Puritans in the White House"? Or really anybody or anything not imagined by Sartre?

Politically, Sartre is revolutionary. Freedom, in affirming itself "must" affirm it for others. The force of the "must" here is unclear. In any event, Sartre sees the political consequences of his affirmation of the freedom of man in a society sketched along Marxist lines. Sartre reads Marx not through Stalinist-Trotskyite eyes but rather as teaching for the first time that we are beholden neither to tradition nor to existing structures of class, property ownership, or consumption and that we are free to make our own history. We need only come to a consciousness of our enslaved condition, of the changeability of every situation in which we thought we had been caught, to see that we have been accepting under the title of "necessary" a society which is degrading. His own existentialism can supply the solid philosophical foundation for a genuinely revolutionary movement within these Marxist outlines. It goes almost without saying that the French communists have a certain uneasiness about founding their own projects upon Sartre's philosophy of freedom, with Sartre's denunciation of Soviet behavior in Hungary, and, in general, about this philosopher who seems to be urging a course of political advance close to their own but sufficiently different to enable him to scoff at their "philosophy," their "sclerotic" sense of party conformity and bureaucracy and their insufficient respect for human freedom. What is clear, however, is Sartre's incorrigible hatred for the "bourgeoisie." *Nausea,* his first novel, gives us a view of them: so many fakes, pompous, inflated, self-righteous, and solid. They are the respectable "city fathers," and they all more or less resemble Daumier's portraits, their humanity and anxiety smothered in self-congratulation, in smugness, "maturity," and the sense of being on the side of God, Nature, Evolution, and Progress. Fidel Castro, on the other hand, is a Sartrean hero, having revealed the alterability of the Cuban situation to his people, showing them by acts that the sugar quota established by the "Puritans in the White House" under orders from the American sugar industry was not established by God, was not necessary, and that the whole order of things could be changed. There is no mention however in *Sartre on Cuba* of Castro's executions without trial, shootings upon mere allegation of crimes or from mistakes in names.[7] All in all, while

[7] *Sartre on Cuba* (New York, 1961). For an unfavorable report on Sartre's political twistings and turnings, see the scathing article by the Swiss writer Herbert Lüthy, "The Void of Jean-Paul Sartre," in *The Anchor Review* #2 (Garden City, 1957), pp. 241 ff.

Sartre has some fresh and perceptive things to say about the passing political scene, it is not his best theme. Ontological studies are not always the most appropriate preparation for historical judgments; and if there is a clear and absolute opposition between Being and Nothingness, it is far from being clear that Cuba and the United States or France and the Soviet Union are related in any such manner. Sartre writes frequently and rapidly on political subjects in a style designed to suggest that the opposition to his views must be composed of either fools or knaves; on the whole it verges on the worst of journalism.

In a word, an extraordinarily provocative thinker of very uneven merits. In the first place, he writes too much or throws away too little. As a consequence, his works have the same interminability which we should expect from a consciousness which was conscious only insofar as it negated itself. Secondly, there is only an apparent coherence of view. It would be very easy to exaggerate his consistency and lucidity. For one thing, on the most abstract dialectical level, he defines God as a contradiction; but we had just finished reading his defense of contradiction, in which he makes contradiction itself the very central core of consciousness! The conclusion in school logic would be that God exists as consciousness, but Sartre's contention is that there is no such thing at all. Hegel, of whom Sartre is something of a caricature, was at least consistent in this respect. If the spirit is negation, the other side of negation is a recuperation; and God is the infinite eternal spirit forever self-alienated, forever self-recuperating. And again: Sartre insists that man has no essence, that he is absolute freedom in a situation, and even that a "solitary drunkard is of equal value with a leader of the nation." Yet he forgets all this when treating Jean Genet, declaring that Genet has cut himself off from both his body and from nature and society, at which point Sartre's bourgeois sensibilities recoil. Sartre's "lucidity"? One need only read his descriptions of erotic love and his analyses of the "friendship of the bourgeoisie for its excrements" to see the source.[8] There are very few writers who can so thoroughly disgust themselves with their own themes, and Sartre's *method* is clear; all he need do is turn a clinical detachment upon the caress, or a couple in bed, for it to become hideous. *Objectification* is the technique, a withholding of any participative sympathy. In *Nausea*, he finds himself looking *at* his hand; it becomes senseless and obscene, a mere thing. Sartre continues to practice this attitude, showing acts in a light which would horrify the participants; he refuses participation in them and then holds up the corpse for our disgust. But then there are acts to which he arbitrarily refuses this objectification; here he counts on the success of rhetoric in already having won us over to his sympathies. The "worker," the "revolutionary," "Fidel Castro"—these occupy the field of his real sympathies; they are "efficacious." As we know from the memoirs of Simone de Beauvoir, Sartre himself has always longed to become "efficacious"; instead, the workers regard him as an "intellectual." They know nothing of Being and Nothingness; but Sartre talks of little else. And finally, to

[8] *Saint Genet,* p. 231.

conclude the list of his faults, his mind is almost destined to misunderstand the concrete. His "existentialism" was offered as a movement of the spirit which could at last avoid principles, laws, essences, universals, and return to existence as singularly and socially lived. It presented itself in Kierkegaard and Nietzsche not as a new theory but as a return of the spirit from classical philosophy to life; let us take our positions where we are anyway, as existing men, for whom life is not a problem to be solved theoretically but something to be lived. And so Sartre *says;* but his philosophy effects the contrary result. This essentially Cartesian spirit, longing for existence, fascinated with thieves and homosexuals, envying the practical problems of workers, endeavors to give us a new *theory* of it all. Descending from the specious clarity of Being and Nothingness, he sees in human existence only that which it offers by way of example *for that theory.* If there seems to be an eternal logical opposition between Being and Nothingness, between the Object and the Subject, Sartre sees in existence only that which it might seem to offer by way of illustration. Human life is a futility, desire never reaches its object, Baudelaire wanted to become a human mineral, Jean Genet wants to be a saint, morality is both necessary and impossible, human existence is a futile passion, etc. But this is nothing less than the spirit of abstraction. Hence Sartre is wonderful in his cartoons of human life but unconvincing if these images are presented as truth.

A philosophy which looks at life as Sartre's does —and not all do—cannot commence with a dialectical proposition in the domain of ontology; it can only begin with concrete life itself and let whatever ontology is necessary emerge from a sympathetic and lucid analysis of life. A caricature of life is at the same time an error, and an error of substantial effect. The attempt to *prove* that there is no love, only a crumbling illusion which fades into either sadism or masochism, can be an amusing danger; the demonstration that man must be a futile passion again strikes a passing echo in our souls, but then is it the truth? Sartre has on his side the current mood that *any* form of affirmation of love or of man must be a species of self-deception and humbuggery. Still, it is hardly necessary to fall in love with the Establishment, with the "bourgeoisie," with "conformism" or the Church to oppose Sartre. Too often, it is obvious, he has not deeply enough understood his opposition.

All which would be more forgivable if pervading the whole of Sartre's writing there were not an ineffable *pride*. There seldom seems to be a shadow of a doubt in Sartre; and when there is, it is but a shadow, offered as more or less excusable for being confessed. But of any sense of reverence, awe, mystery, or humility, there is none. All such sentiments are *perimées* and belong to the domain of private subjectivity at home in a society of aristocratic consumption; they have no "efficacity." And indeed it is hard to defend them in a debate on Union Square; what good do they do? Nevertheless, for whatever final, open atmosphere they might supply to our judgments of one another and of life, they are certainly absent in the works of Jean-Paul Sartre.

Why then bother to read him? And here I find myself in the same position as Sartre with his prayer for treating Jean Genet well. To be *convinced* by

Sartre would be a disaster. And yet to ignore him altogether would be to miss an essential truth. In effect, Sartre is important as a thinker to be overcome, but not exactly through the alternatives *he* presents. His own philosophy, his own sentiment of human existence is intolerable and false; and yet any other philosophy which is not *more* lucid or *more* faithful to life is unimportant. Sartre is very, very far from being a fool; but his philosophy is also far from being either finally true or even thinkable.

In the end what is at issue here? There are a number of ways of putting it: the concrete versus the abstract (but this is itself a distinction floating among abstractions); the sentiment of fidelity versus the passion for revolution (but who can be anything but revolutionary?); or eventually, Being versus Nothingness. Sartre is obsessed with Being; for him it is a *settling*, a solidification, the past, very much like the Alps for Hegel, who found them boring simply because they were there; and Sartre finds that consciousness is nothing but a flight *from* such Being. But then is there not a being to the flight; for even if it constitutes our life, that life is a something lived, and the word Nothingness seems hardly the last thing to be said about it. And yet, there is the perpetual temptation to forget this endless flight, this endless nothingness of our lives, and surreptitiously live in the sentiment that there is no nothingness at all, that, after all, the essential things have been settled. We have been settled, our society has been settled, our truth has been settled, and our loves settled. Here Sartre punctures the balloon. At bottom Sartre is an inverted platonic metaphysician who keeps one eye cocked on the hated eternity of mere being while he is at the same time fascinated by the endless explosiveness and becoming of our lives.

In my own opinion he is not a wise man, and with this he would most assuredly agree; no one hates what has passed for wisdom more than Sartre. But then the dispute is not so simple as this, and it is indispensable to read Sartre in order to recover some sense of what is missing, a wisdom which is neither a perpetual flight from being anything nor a settling into a type or into a cartoon of a human being, a wisdom which has its heart set neither on conformity to what is nor onto such fatuous ideals as the dream of a workers' community. To attempt to freeze into a Being which Sartre so rightly loathes is unwise, and it is also unwise to live in perpetual defiance of being anything, always remaking one's bed. The truth is more that, while these particular oppositions all have their utility in characterizing certain stages of our development, neither Sartre nor what he presents as his opposition is viable. In a word, human wisdom for whatever it is worth lies in neither place, but may perhaps be reinvigorated by opposition to Sartre and the Sartre which is ourselves.

WILLIAM EARLE

V / The Absence of God

(HEIDEGGER AND TILLICH)

Towards the middle of the nineteenth century Western philosophers of religion began to challenge Christianity with a new type of argument, the historical critique. Whereas the philosophers of earlier periods had argued against (or defended) Christianity as a *doctrine*, it now began to be attacked *as an historical experience*. Atheistic philosophers ceased exhausting themselves in the impossible task of demonstrating that God does not exist and, instead, attempted to show how the idea of God could arise in the first place. This is the so-called "historical refutation" of Christianity which Nietzsche considered "the only definitive one." We have already seen, in the first chapter, how Kierkegaard also moved Christian philosophy to the plane of historical experience, and we will return to the "Christian" experience later in this chapter. Here it is less a question of pitting Christians against atheists than of trying to see how both have posed the problem of religion as an existential and experiential concern. This is characteristic of contemporary thought; in fact we can say that contemporary philosophy *begins* in the momentous questioning of the Christian experience by philosophers like Feuerbach, Nietzsche, Kierkegaard, Dostoevsky, and Freud in the second half of the nineteenth century.

The argument of Feuerbach and Nietzsche, in simplified form, runs something like this. God is the ideal or the mirror of man. All those divine and holy attributes which mankind has placed in God as unattainable ideals, his goodness, mercy, compassion, pity, love, wisdom, justice, and so on, are in reality "human" qualities, human experiences. Man has fashioned a God in his own image and likeness. And because man experiences *himself* as less-than-good, less-than-merciful, less-than-just, he feels there must somehow, somewhere exist that perfect being which he himself *is not* but which he obscurely and at rare, exceptional, exalted moments desires *to become*. In short, what man has worshipped is the idea of *the perfect man*, placed by imagination in an inaccessible and unattainable realm "beyond" this world. But this very worship of an imaginary "human" ideal has had a debilitating effect on mankind. By situating God outside the world, outside man himself, the effort of progressively improving man himself, the human condition here below, has been weakened. What is great, noble, exalted in human experience is called *God*. What is weak, miserable, pitiful is called *man*. *Man* thus remains in a state of lethargy and is content to "blame God" for his moral and

material weakness. He has remained, under the influence of religion, less than human, less than he
could become. And, according to Nietzsche, Christianity represents the worst case of all. It is a "la-
mentable story" of men inventing a principle (God)
in the name of which they can despise man, of inventing another world in order to calumniate this one.
It is now time for man to re-enter into the possession
of the higher qualities of which Christianity has dis-
possessed him. We must choose against Christianity
in order to liberate man; we must return to the earth.

In announcing this message Nietzsche and other
nineteenth-century thinkers adopted an apocalyptic,
"scriptural" tone. The poet Heine gives the *vita* of
the God whom the Christians gave to Europe in the
following words:

> Our hearts are thrilled with compassion, for it is old
> Jehovah himself who is making ready to die. We have
> known him so well, from his cradle in Egypt, where
> he was brought up among the divine crocodiles and
> calves, the onions and ibises and sacred cats. . . . We
> saw him bid farewell to those companions of his
> childhood, the obelisks and sphinxes of the Nile, to
> become a little god-king in Palestine to a poor nation
> of shepherds. . . . Later we saw him in contact with
> the Assyro-Babylonian civilization; at that stage he
> gave up his far too human passions and refrained
> from spitting wrath and vengeance; at any rate, he
> no longer thundered for the least trifle. . . . We saw
> him move to Rome, the capital, where he abjured
> everything in the way of national prejudice and pro-
> claimed the celestial equality of all peoples; with
> these fine phrases he set up in opposition to old
> Jupiter, and, thanks to intriguing, he got into power

and, from the heights of the Capital, ruled the city and the world, *urbem et orbem*. . . . We have seen him purify himself, spiritualize himself still more, become paternal, compassionate, the benefactor of the human race, a philanthropist. . . . But nothing could save him! Don't you hear the bell? Down on your knees! The sacrament is being carried to a dying God."[1]

In *Zarathustra* Nietzsche tells the story with less irony but more passion; this God of the Christians became, with age, more and more piti-ful, and he ended by suffocating himself in an excess of pity for the human race. In short the Christian God revealed himself to be the product of a piteous, weak, sick civilization. "The Christian conception of God—God as god of the sick, God as a spider . . . ," he vomits.[2]

I *condemn* Christianity. I raise against the Christian church the most terrible of all accusations that any accuser ever uttered. It is to me the highest of all conceivable corruptions. It has had the will to the last corruption that is even possible. The Christian church has left nothing untouched by its corruption; it has turned every value into an un-value, every truth into a lie, every integrity into a vileness of the soul.[3]

This "religion of pity" has corrupted the con-

[1] Heinrich Heine, "De l'Allemagne depuis Luther," in *Revue des Deux-Mondes*, IV (1834), 408, as quoted in Henri De Lubac, *The Drama of Atheist Humanism*, trans. Edith M. Riley (New York, 1950), pp. 21–22.

[2] Friedrich Nietzsche, *The Antichrist*, trans. Walter Kaufmann, *The Portable Nietzsche*, (New York, 1954), p. 585.

[3] *Ibid.*, p. 655.

science of Western man and denatured "the strong races of northern Europe."[4] Though his language is the most extreme and relentless of all, Nietzsche was only one of the spokesmen of a common judgment on Christian civilization as it existed at the end of the nineteenth century. Whether we turn to Christians like Kierkegaard and Dostoevsky or to anti-Christians like Nietzsche and Feuerbach, we find essentially the same judgment of condemnation: the institutions of Christianity are corrupt and lifeless. Man "has got lost" and is now alone in the world. "I have got lost; I am everything that has got lost, sighs modern man."[5]

In short, the nineteenth century was the period of the death of God in Western Christian civilization. Nietzsche presents man as the "assassin" of God; Dostoevsky presents him as the "parricide." It is into this post-Christian era that Heidegger and Tillich emerged *as philosophers.* We will turn presently to their appraisal of the human condition in this post-Nietzschean world.

What did the late nineteenth century do to religion and, therefore, to man? What is this world that contemporary thinkers have inherited? It killed God. This "great happening" which drove the sensitive and, in spite of himself, still-Christian Nietzsche to despair and ultimately to madness was faced by only a few at first. Not only Nietzsche but Dostoevsky and Kierkegaard also ended their lives in a condition which suggests that the "burden" of their message was heavier and more terrible than any single mind

[4] *Ibid.,* p. 586.

[5] *Ibid.,* p. 569.

could bear. It has been suggested that, as prophets, they acted out the frightening psychosis which was beginning to take hold of the European mind. The period of Nietzsche has been called the Good Friday of Western philosophy.

The theme of the Death of God, in itself, was not new to Christianity; as a boy Nietzsche must often have sung Luther's chorale "God Himself Is Dead." But God, in the New Testament, died only to prove that he could *not* die, and Christianity had been sustained by the hope of resurrection for nineteen hundred years. Now Nietzsche gives the Death of God a new sense.

> Whither is God? . . . I shall tell you. *We have killed him*—you and I. All of us are his murderers. . . . God is dead. God remains dead. And we have killed him. How shall we, the murderers of all murderers, comfort ourselves? What was holiest and most powerful of all that the world has yet owned has bled to death under our knives. Who will wipe this blood off us?[6]

But Nietzsche knew that he had arrived too soon, that it would take centuries for this terrible "truth" to be realized, that it would be centuries before the shadow of God disappeared from the walls of the caves in which the mass of humanity dwells. The sun is already setting, but it still illumines our lives in the twilight. The experience of the Death of God, the *Gottestode*, has brought us to the twilight of the world (*Weltverdüsterung*). In the nineteenth century mankind definitely turned from God to technology and the power of "science" for salvation. The

[6] Friedrich Nietzsche, *The Gay Science*, loc. cit., p. 95.

Absolute, which had formerly been situated beyond the sensible world is now relocated here, on this side of the beyond, in the world, in man.

For Feuerbach and Nietzsche this is the simple constatation of a fact. God is dead even if men are still unaware of it and continue to frequent the caves, even if their guilt as "assassins" and the enormity of what has happened has not yet penetrated to the level of their conscious awareness. But Nietzsche is Feuerbach *plus passion;* man, indeed, is liberated and free at last to become himself, but in Nietzsche's writings the *Gottestode* is not the basis for a new and consoling "humanism." It is a frightening experience which is just beginning. Man has for so long conditioned himself to placing all that is great and noble, all that is of the spirit, in the "beyond" that he is now unable to "inherit the earth" which he himself has impoverished. Man is entering the period of the dictatorship of "objective" science and mechanical techniques; the forces of spiritual creativity are becoming weaker; we are assisting at the decline of the spirit in Western civilization, the period of the *Entmachtung des Geistes.* As a result men have become "superficial" and "impotent." Where they ought now to face the task of creating man, they are content to invent machines and to mask their failure with "the spirit of gravity." Worst of all, men have lost control over technology and over the irrational forces which have now begun to "play" with mankind.

Nietzsche is the prophet *of* and *to* the dying nineteenth century, the Crystal Palace rationalism of the Victorian era, the civilization which irrationally destroyed itself in the holocaust of 1914–1918, fought out on the soil of the two most "civilized" nations of Europe, Germany and France. After that catastrophe and what followed, the whole direction of European philosophy was forceably changed. Philosophers were suddenly faced with the world which Nietzsche had predicted. Contemporary philosophers, to transpose a strong metaphor of William Barrett, are now faced with the laborious task of digging their way out of the Nietzschean ruins, like survivors out of a bombed city.[7] But contemporary philosophy remains Nietzschean; the historical experience which Nietzsche described is still developing, and there is no turning back. We are entering the night of the world. It is this world of spiritual darkness which Heidegger, the disciple of Hölderlin, describes.

Heidegger's philosophy of man is a philosophy of radical human finitude. It has been called a description of the world *from which God is absent*. It is Heidegger who has given to modern theology its problem of the "silence of God." As a young man, in a Jesuit Scholasticate in Freiburg, Heidegger underwent a sharp religious crisis—the Nietzschean crisis—*the* crisis of the twentieth-century religious mind. He has intimated that he experienced the Death of God.[8] And we know that he *lived through*

[7] William Barrett, *Irrational Man* (New York, 1962), p. 205.

[8] "Because reference is made to Nietzsche's expression of 'God's death,' one declares such a procedure to be atheism. For what is more 'logical' than that one who has experienced 'God's death' is a godless person?" (Martin Heidegger, *Letter on Humanism*, trans. Edgar Lohner, in *Philosophy in the Twentieth Century*, ed. Henry D. Aiken and William Barrett [New York, 1962], II, 291). Cf. also William Barrett, *Irrational Man*, p. 209.

the experience without, however, becoming an atheist. My thought, he writes calmly, "can no more be theistic than it can be atheistic."[9] The question of God is simply no longer posed, not because of "indifference" but "out of respect for *the limits which have been set* upon thought as thought."[10] Heidegger has followed Nietzsche's advice to "return to the earth" and has elaborated a philosophy of man-in-the-world, of man-on-this-side-of-the-divine. Philosophy, says Heidegger, no longer has the right to pose questions concerning *the eternal,* and the divine, *Die Gottheit.* In order to understand itself, it must first try to *think* the historical, contingent, finite experience which is its only route of access to "the truth of Being."

> In so far as thought does not exceed the limits of its task, *at the moment of present world destiny* it gives man an indication of the original dimension of his *historical abode.* In so far as thought expresses in this way the truth of Being, it has entrusted itself to what is more essential than all values and all beings. Thought does not overcome metaphysics by surpassing and cancelling it in some direction or other and ascending even higher: *it descends* into the nearness of the nearest.[11]

Thus, Heidegger's philosophy is *necessarily* a philosophy of the human condition, a *descent* to the experiential foundations of being rather than an ascent to the eternal. It is an *anthropology,* a phi-

[9] Martin Heidegger, *Letter on Humanism, op. cit.,* p. 294.

[10] *Ibid.;* italics mine.

[11] *Ibid.;* italics mine.

losophy of "time-bound," "earth-bound" man. Heidegger rejects all former metaphysics as a painful
experience, and hence he will not attempt to decide
anything "about the existence or non-existence of
God any more than about the possibility or impossibility of the gods."[12] The very meaning of such
questions has become obscured and is no longer
clear. Before they can, perhaps, one day be asked
again, it is necessary to clarify the truth of Being.
At the present time it is impossible for man "to ask
seriously and firmly whether God approaches or
withdraws."

> Only from the truth of Being can the essence of the
> holy be thought. Only from the essence of the holy
> can the essence of the divinity be thought. Only in
> the light of the essence of the divinity can it be
> thought and said what the word "God" is to signify.
> Or must we not first be able to understand and hear
> these words carefully if we as men, i.e. as existing
> beings, are to have the privilege of experiencing a
> relation of God to man? . . . *Perhaps the distinction
> of this age consists in the fact that the dimension of
> grace has been closed. Perhaps this is its unique
> dis-grace.*[13]

Note the future tense. Heidegger does not say
"what the word *God* means" but what it "is to sig-
nify." Such a question is now premature. Man must
wait. Heidegger describes a world "waiting for God."
This silence of God, this absence of grace, and the
consequent inutility of even attempting to pose the

[12] *Ibid.*, p. 293. Note here an error in Mr. Lohner's trans-
lation of this sentence which I have corrected.

[13] *Ibid.*, p. 294.

question of man's possible relation to God penetrates contemporary thought and literature. It is present in André Gide, Albert Camus, Simone Weil, Jean-Paul Sartre. Ingmar Bergman's *Through a Glass Darkly* and the plays of Samuel Beckett convey the same message. In *Waiting for Godot* the religious frustration is evident. This play is structured around an appointed meeting with Godot ("God"?) which never takes place. Vladimir and Estragon wait, they attempt *to remember*, to imagine something they seem to have known or surmised dimly but have forgotten. They wait, in obscurity, fatigue, weakness and indecisiveness, without knowledge and really without hope, with only a vague, childish trust that Godot will come and explain the *meaning* of their waiting to them. And in the meantime they do nothing at all, "because it is more prudent."[14]

The Christians, says Sartre, have claimed that there is a divine plan for man and that God has revealed it. Yet, nobody seems to have got the message straight, and no one really knows whether God will keep his rendezvous with the human race. The Christians are divided, and no two of them interpret God's message in the same way. Yet, if God is all-powerful, he must have the means of making himself understood and of leading men to salvation, even without their own gauche and ineffectual assistance. At any event, even granting that the Christians are right, that there *are* signs, each man is left alone to interpret them for himself on his own responsibility. And in the meantime Christians live their lives on the same evidence as everybody else. "Even if God

[14] Samuel Beckett, *En attendant Godot* (Paris, 1952), p. 27 and *passim.*

existed, that would change nothing. . . . Man must rediscover himself and persuade himself that nothing can save him from himself, not even a valid proof of the existence of God."[15]

Heidegger's philosophy is, therefore, an attempt to *think* once again, starting from the beginning, the truth of Being. In the post-Nietzschean world this is a difficult task. Men, and philosophers as well, have given themselves over so completely to "speaking" and "doing" that they have forgotten how to "be silent" and "to listen." But if man does not listen, Being will not be heard. It is not that Being does not speak to man but rather that its voice cannot be heard above the din of technology. In order to rediscover the truth of Being, we must cease trying to manipulate beings and let Being *be*. But what is Being? What is truth? And how are we to approach the truth of Being?

Since we cannot appeal to grace or escape from our condition as men to discover our answers already inscribed on some supernatural blueprint, we must necessarily begin with a description—a phenomenological description—of the experience of modern man. Hiedegger is a phenomenologist who never approaches Being or truth except *from experience*. His most important book, *Being and Time*, is thus an attempt to elaborate a new anthropology, a new theory of man and human life in the first post-Christian century, an investigation which is neither theistic nor atheistic but which is situated at a level on which such "derived" questions cannot yet be posed. It is first of all a description of the *being* of man. In

[15] Jean-Paul Sartre, *L'existentialisme* (Paris, 1957), p. 95.

this first sense "being" means *existence,* and Heidegger gives us a new description of human existence as *Dasein.* Literally, *Dasein* means to-be-there. But Heidegger does not take this in an impersonal, "objective" sense. *Dasein* also, and primarily, means *to-be-present.* Man is a conscious *presence* to himself, to other men, and to the world. *Ek-sistence* is an *ek-stasis,* which means that it is a "standing-outside-itself" in the world in the presence of others. My being is not something that is confined within the physical contours of my body; it includes the "field" or region of being *to which I am present.* My existence is not a monadic self-containment but a centrifugal, world-directed force, an action and a *praxis.* Heidegger's theory of man is thus a "field-theory" of man's being-in-the-world which is a temporal as well as a spatial *ek-stasis.* But it is more than that; human existence is essentially *the field of human meaning and care.* I *am* everywhere my care and concern for the world make themselves felt.

Heidegger's *existential analysis* of man thus begins with the total complexity of the concrete, existing individual. His first consideration is that man *actually exists* as an emerging, becoming, self-transcending reality. Being, for Heidegger, is not to be understood, in a Greek sense, as static, necessary, unchanging, eternal; it is essentially historical. Time, he says, is "the ontological meaning of care," which is to say of human existence. Man's existence is *extended* not only in space but also, and primarily, in time. Human life is never concentrated in the present; man also lives in the past and, especially, in the future. He experiences his temporality and his future-directedness. The true *meaning* of a man's

life lies ahead of him, always in the future, in projects which are *not yet* achieved. Man is not a historical being primarily because he is necessarily im-
plicated in the vast, ongoing, irrevocable historical
process, because he must live in his century, adopt
the manners and wear the clothes of his epoch, and
so on. This is a folkloristic notion of time. Man is
historical as the *source* of history; it is he who gives
definition and direction to life and thus gives to *be-ing*
a meaning. The unconscious processes, the inarticu-
late flux of happenings become history in man. All
human life is a leap into the *not-yet* of the future.
Man is therefore, says Heidegger, defined by *nothing*,
surrounded by *nothing*. For, if we say that existence
is temporal, we say that it is *finite*, penetrated and
surrounded by *nothingness*, that is, by time.

Given this notion of time, not as the locus or
condition of existence, but as its intrinsic ontological
structure, we can now attempt to understand what
Heidegger means by being and nothingness. It is
best to approach this question, as Heidegger approached it in *Being and Time*, through a study of
some of the existential (and therefore intrinsically
historical) structures of human existence, such as
Death, Freedom, Authenticity, Dread, Care, Guilt, Resolve, and so on. It is not possible here to give a
detailed account of Heidegger's anthropology; we
must limit ourselves to a few hints concerning the
scope of his analysis. The analysis itself is called
Dasein-analytics or *existential analysis*. This is not
only to distinguish it from other forms of philosophical analysis, such as formal or logical analysis for
example, but also to distinguish it from the kind of
description of existence we find in the earlier exis-

tentialists. Very few of the "existential" categories
which Heidegger discusses were not already discovered and described by Dostoevsky, Kierkegaard,
Nietzsche, and others. But these writers limited
themselves to the description of concrete situations
in which such experiences occur. Heidegger goes
beyond what he calls this existenti*el* description to
an existenti*al* or *ontological* investigation. He is trying to make explicit the fundamental categories of
lived existence as such. These are not "attributes"
of man to be used in making definitions, nor is Heidegger attempting to give us an exhaustive list of
existential categories. Each "category" represents a
new effort to *think* what is most fundamental in
human existence *as such*. Each one expresses or
"thematizes" the totality of human existence—*totum
sed non totaliter*—under one of its aspects. What
are some of these categories, and what do they
mean?

Heidegger has written a lot on Death and Free-
dom-towards-death. Some of his early readers, particularly in this country and England, took him con-
sequently for a morbid man, preoccupied with the
unpleasantness of human life to the exclusion of
any optimism or "humanism" at all. It is true that
all the existentialist writers, and in this Heidegger
is an "existentialist," have taken a very *serious* view
of what man has become. They do not emphasize
glorious, triumphant rationality, man the Baconian
hero, nor do they repeat the "What a wonderful
creature is man" of the early nineteenth-century
humanists. Against the fatuous optimism of the "humanism" of the nineteenth century, existentialists
sometimes seem to take delight in awakening their

contemporaries to the true "human condition." Nietzsche said that after the creation of man "the old God
was seized with a hellish fear" because "man himself had turned out to be his *greatest* mistake," and
his own conclusion was that "man is something
which must be overcome." Sartre has defined man
as a "useless passion" restlessly and blindly striving
—against an ontological impossibility—to become
God.[16] But Heidegger, for his part, is not out to vilify
human nature or to attack the dignity of man. His
desire is to see human existence clearly, as it reveals
itself *in reality*. No philosopher has been more preoccupied with discovering the dignity and freedom
of human existence than Heidegger. It is, nevertheless, disconcerting to hear him announce that this
dignity and freedom is rooted in the experience of
Death and Nothingness. But what does he mean?

The Death of which Heidegger speaks is not my
own, little, empirical end, which in any case I have
not yet experienced and thus cannot describe. Nor
is it the "objective fact" of death. It is rather the
Death that is *me,* that is an *intrinsic possibility* of
my own present being. Death as an immanent potentiality of the *Dasein* reveals to me the radical finitude of my existence. And, says Heidegger, this revelation has a *liberating character*.[17] It frees me *from*

[16] Friedrich Nietzsche, *The Antichrist, loc. cit.,* p. 629;
Thus Spoke Zarathustra, ibid., p. 379. Jean-Paul Sartre,
L'être et le néant (Paris, 1943), p. 708.

[17] Martin Heidegger, *Being and Time,* trans. John Mac-
quarrie and Edward Robinson (New York, 1962), pp. 293,
ff, 302 ff. The following references to *Being and Time* are
not meant as exhaustive documentation for the extremely
synthetic statement of Heidegger's thought offered here but
only as a help to the general reader unacquainted with Heidegger's text.

the mean, the petty, the narrow, the unauthentic, and it frees me *for* awareness, responsibility, freedom, authentic existence. The nothingness of Death is present within my being as one of its intrinsic structures; it is always there, like a mole, underneath the calm surface preoccupation with my daily affairs. It is inseparable from myself and is the source of both my radical anxiety and of my freedom.

This is both an ontological and an ethical structure. Being, as it is experienced by me, *my being*, is headed for death. This is not to be understood exclusively as the end of my life but also as the death which I die each day, each time I make a moral choice, at each moment, as the present slips into the past and thus irrevocably escapes my control. It is by assuming the "nothingness" of my existence that I come to *myself*, that I realize finally the seriousness of my existence, that I become an *authentic self*. Ordinarily, men live in a state of "forgetfulness" or "oblivion" of their being. They are lost in the impersonal and public world of *Das Man*, and it is only by assuming the "truth" of their being that they can become fully men. Death is thus a structure of awareness. Ultimately, what Death reveals is that our lives are radically our own; we cannot shift the responsibility onto anyone else. No man can think for another, no man can experience in the place of another. To attempt to do so is a denial of human existence, a flight from responsibility, a refusal to *become* human. Human lives are not interchangeable. Men who attempt to let others think *for* them, whether they be their theologians, their politicians, their newspapermen, their heroes, are existential *cowards*.[18] Authentic existence requires a courage to accept the experience of nothingness which is within us, a *Mut zur Angst,* to accept ourselves as free, responsible, historical.

The experience of Dread or Anxiety (*Angst*), particularly in the form of *ethical anxiety* (i.e., responsibility for choices which must always be made without full "knowledge") reveals another aspect of the existential structure of human existence.[19] Dread, as an ontological structure of human reality, has nothing directly to do with fear or worry. Dread is not the focused, explicit fear of *something,* but an uncanny, pervasive, subliminal fear of *nothing,* a fear that creeps up from behind. It is a fear of not-being, an ontologically present fear in the lived awareness that we could not-be. Anxiety is experienced when we cease being *Das Man* and become *Dasein,* authentically present to the world as a human freedom. This is a dread of *nothing,* it is a man's anxiety over his own unlimited and undetermined *possibility,* of what he *could become,* of what he could *have* become. In an existence which is radically contingent, radically finite, everything *could be* other than it is, and man above all. Since this existential anxiety is an essential structure of human existence, contemporary psychoanalysts who have

[18] Cf. Sartre, *L'existentialisme,* pp. 84–85: "Those who hide from their total freedom, in a guise of solemnity or with deterministic excuses, I shall call *cowards;* those who try to show that their existence is necessary, when it is merely an accident of the appearance of the human race on earth, I shall call *scum*" (trans. Philip Mairet, with slight modifications; italics mine).

[19] *Being and Time,* pp. 227 ff.

been influenced by Heidegger no longer make it
their goal to free man *from* anxiety, understood in
this sense, but rather to free man *for* anxiety, to
live *with* anxiety. A man who is *not at all* anxious
is less than human, and the thought of Heidegger
has given a new meaning to the "age of anxiety" in
which we live. For existential psychoanalysis the
categories of Anxiety, Dread, Death are dimensions
of human existence which cannot be escaped. Man
is, as Sartre says, "condemned to be free." If a man
takes flight from his radical freedom to escape into
a "false" world of neurosis or insanity, the job of
the psychoanalyst is to lead him, in so far as possible, back to the point where he can again exercise
his freedom to be himself *with* anxiety.

If the correlate of Dread is "nothingness," the
correlate of Care (*Sorge*) is "being."[20] Man, says Heidegger, is "'thrown" into the world. He did not ask
to be there; he *finds himself* gradually amidst the
facticity of worldly experience. Man lives "in the
midst of things" which he did not create and for
which he is not responsible. But man's typical relationship to being is *Care*. He assumes a responsibility for beings; he creates science and technology;
he gives the world a "human" meaning. In short,
man is *concerned* about the beings of the world; he
is like the "shepherd" of beings and he tries to *comprehend* them in the double sense of "keeping them
together" and of "understanding" them. Heidegger
has rooted the primary phenomena of speech, feeling, understanding, and thought in this primal concern of man for beings. Man did not create the hu-

[20] *Ibid.*, pp. 225 ff.

man situation; he finds it. There is a brute given-
ness, a dumb and inescapable "facticity" about existence which man can overcome (Heidegger says
"climb over" as one climbs over obstacles) only little
by little, partially, and with great effort. It is difficult to *think* being, but this is man's typical response
to his existence. It is what defines man as man and
distinguishes him from other "beings" who must
dumbly accept their "situation," forever remaining
beneath the level of "caring" about it.

Finally, let us briefly mention the categories of
Guilt and Resolve.[21] Again, the sense of Guilt here
is not that of the guilt-feelings of abnormal psychology. In German the word for "Guilt" is related
to "Debt" and "Responsibility." Man is not entirely
"his own being." He lives in an intersubjective world;
his experience imposes on him "debts" to others.
He owes his very existence to others, and his "care
for beings" would not and could not be exercised
except in the company of others, *for others*. This
nevertheless imposes the great responsibility for
human history, for human culture, for human society on the shoulders of man. No man can escape
his "guilt" (i.e., responsibility) for others, and to
"blame God" for the human condition is a gratuitous
and unheroic attempt to escape from reality. But
authentic human existence, says Heidegger, is Resolute. Existence is a dynamic, future-oriented, ongoing activity. It is not a simple biological *process*
which operates of itself but a deliberate action. The
resolute man is the valuator, the giver of direction
and meaning to being. Man transcends his situation

[21] *Ibid.*, pp. 314 ff., 325 ff., 342 ff.

by "knowing" it and giving it "value." This human resolve or intention to confer meaning on being is, of course, a very precarious, partial, eternally incomplete, revisable *project*. In this sense the view of man which emerges from Heidegger's Dasein-analytics is highly "Faustian." But, since God is Dead, or at least "silent," we have no one to ask for the solution; in this period of "dis-grace" man is not only free but is forced, to create, to invent, to strive to transcend himself and his situation *alone*.

After giving this very brief summary of some of the results of Heidegger's existential analysis of human reality, we can now turn to the original problem of thinking *the truth of Being*. We have up to now examined the "truth of being" when being is understood as human *existence*. But human reality is, for Heidegger, only our route of access to Being; it is not Being itself. Since we have no other route of access to Being than *existence*, human reality is necessarily the foundation of the "truth" and "value" of being, but it is not the foundation of the *to be* of being, Being itself. To *think* the *Being of being*, this is Heidegger's self-imposed task, which he wants to conduct outside the dead and discarded categories of former metaphysics. The sense he gives to the word "truth" is not that commonly accepted by philosophers ever since Plato defined truth as the correctness of an intellectual judgment in the human mind. Truth (*a-létheia*) in Heidegger's sense will only be found by letting Being unveil itself when we become *present to* it. This presence-to-Being is not the "logical reasoning" within which most of Western philosophy has been conducted. It is an *attending to* Being that involves all man's powers at once. It is more of a "listening" to Being than an attempt to conquer Being in a Baconian manner or to rob Being of its secrets.

> Man ought, before speaking, once more let Being speak to him, at the risk of having little or nothing to say in answer to this call. Only thus is it possible to restore to the Word its essential value and to man the privilege of dwelling in the truth of Being.[22]

The whole of Western metaphysics, says Heidegger, has been "the forgetting of Being" (*Vergessenheit des Seins*). Why have men fallen into this total oblivion of Being? Because, says Heidegger, they have been preoccupied with "ontic" knowledge rather than "ontological" thought. Men have been so taken up with "beings" that they have forgotten the *Being* of beings. By "ontic" knowledge Heidegger means the whole gamut of the "sciences" from geometry to theology which man has created to help him understand and control the world, all the moral, artistic and religious institutions he has invented as well, all the *entia* or "beings" with which he is concerned. Man is easily *lost* in ontic reality; he becomes absorbed with "beings" and can no longer attend to Being, the ontological foundation of "beings." In

---

[22] Martin Heidegger, *Über den Humanismus* (Berne, 1947), pp. 60–61. For Heidegger's notion of "truth," cf. *Plato's Doctrine of Truth,* trans. John Barlow for *Philosophy in the Twentieth Century, op. cit.,* pp. 251–70. For Heidegger's later philosophy on the *thought of being,* cf. especially, apart from the works mentioned above, *Vom Wesen der Wahrheit* (Frankfurt, 1943); *Holzwege* (Frankfurt, 1950); *Was heisst Denken?* (Tübingen, 1954); and *Zur Seinsfrage* (Frankfurt, 1956).

answer to the question, What are "beings" as distinct from the Being of beings? we can respond in a Heideggerian way by mentioning the three or four regions of "beings" he has distinguished. There are the "beings" of nature and human culture, the *Zuhandene;* there are the "beings" which are the "objects" of the specular or "objective" sciences, the *Vorhandene;* there are the "beings" of human reality, the *Dasein;* finally there are the gods and divinities, the superhuman realities of "war," "love," "prudence," "fate" and so on. None of these are Being; they are only "beings." Western metaphysics, and later Christian theology, posed the question of the Being of beings in an obscure and faulty manner which nevertheless shows that a real concern for Being lies beneath the history of Western thought. The Christian theologians in particular got close to the *question of Being, the Seinsfrage,* but they also ended by identifying Being with just another "being," even though it was the highest and most "necessary" of all, namely God. Heidegger has told us explicitly that this is not what he means by Being.

> Yet Being—what is Being? It is Itself. Future thought must learn to experience and express this. "Being" is neither God nor the basis of the world. Being is further from all that is being and yet closer to man than every being, be it a rock, an animal, a work of art, a machine, be it an angel or God.[23]

Being is "the closest" to man, and yet "its closeness remains farthest from man" because of man's

[23] *Letter on Humanism,* tr. Edgar Lohner, *op. cit.,* pp. 281–82.

absorbed fascination with "ontic" reality. But the very elaboration of all the human sciences of "beings" ought to show, says Heidegger, that this very preoccupation presupposes a more primitive and more original understanding of the Being of beings. Heidegger is now attempting to lead Western philosophy out of its oblivion of Being to the original problem of Being. Heidegger's meditation on Being is a *Rückgang,* a going-back to the sub-understood and pre-understood ontological foundations of experience which make the human experience of the world a *verstehen,* an understanding. And, this is possible because the *Dasein* as a unitary whole *understands* Being already, though this understanding cannot yet be *said,* cannot be thematized.

> The whole originality of Heidegger is to give its full development to this *Rückgang* which is always in danger of stopping midway, at a Supreme Being, at the World as a Whole, at the Universal Spirit, without seeing that there would be nothing, neither gods, nor world, nor reason, if there were not, before everything else, *that* which permits everything which is to be. . . .[24]

Paul Tillich, the first post-Christian theologian in the Western tradition, was a colleague of Heidegger at the University of Marburg in the 1920's and was strongly influenced by Heidegger's thought. His theology is firmly rooted in the existential categories of Heidegger's Dasein-analytics, though, like his colleague Rudolf Bultmann and the psychiatrist

[24] H. Birault, "Existence et vérité d'après Heidegger," *Revue de métaphysique et de morale* (1951), pp. 39–40.

Ludwig Binswanger, Tillich has continued Heidegger's analysis and made original contributions to it. This has required that he state the problem of God in a new way. Tillich also has lived through the period of the impotence of the forces of the spirit, and he has, with honesty and frankness, accepted the Death of God. To many of his contemporaries, including most Church theologians, Tillich appears as a heroic but enormously confused and embarrassing figure. His tortuous attempt to re-think the Christian message in contemporary, existentialist terms has appeared to many of his fellow theologians as a quixotic and misguided attempt at compromise with a world which should be taken by force, not intrigue. At the same time, non-Christian existentialists and other philosophers have voiced their impatience with this theologian who does not know when to quit. It is not easy to be a theologian in the absence of God. Tillich is the type of man who evoked the puzzlement of Sartre:

> God is dead. Let us not understand by that that he does not exist or even that he no longer exists. He is dead. He spoke to us, and he is silent. We no longer have anything but his cadaver. Perhaps he slipped out of the world, somewhere else, like the soul of a dead man. Perhaps he was only a dream. . . . God is dead, but man has not, for all that, become an atheist.[25]

After philosophers have destroyed the older basis for religious faith, what is left? Only an agonizing religious need, to fill the void. This need is well attested to, as Sartre himself has pointed out, in the

[25] Jean-Paul Sartre, *Situations I* (Paris, 1947), p. 153.

literature and behavior of our contemporaries. It must also be "analyzed," and Tillich has attempted to subject it to an *existential analysis*. In analyzing this *need* for God, Tillich has tried to avoid falling back on the traditional concepts of Christian theology and has, instead, defined God as the response to the "ultimate concern" of the historical and individual human consciousness. The answer to Nietzsche is not to be found in the elaboration of new physical or astronomical proofs for the existence of God; such "natural theology" belongs to an "objectivist" period of thought which has been definitively passed. God is to be reached, if he is reached at all, non-conceptually, in the concrete experience of faith which precedes thought and is independent of any hard thinking, in the divine encounter with self-revealing Being.

We must ask here whether Tillich has simply identified God with Heidegger's *Being of beings,* a step Heidegger had warned against. At first we are almost persuaded that he has. God is not a thing, another being among beings. Tillich has profited from the Heideggerian critique of classical Christian theology, and he no longer simply speaks of "God" but of the "God beyond God," the God who is neither personal nor impersonal but is beyond any conceptual category which man could possibly devise. He is beyond the metaphysical categories of "One" or "Triune," of "Natural" or "Supernatural" and all the others which have caused so much shedding of blood and ink among Christians through history. Tillich is at his best when he is saying what God *is not*, and his criticisms of former theology are clearly as thorough and well-founded as those of

Kierkegaard and Nietzsche. But what is the positive
content of his message? What Tillich has done is
to re-establish God as "beyond" man. This does not
mean, however, that God is to be situated again in
a physical heaven outside the highest sphere. It
means simply that God "transcends" man even in
those experiences in which he reveals himself. It
means that God is never an "object" but *Being*—that
towards which man transcends himself without ever
"reaching" it or "possessing" it. All the attributes of
God discovered so laboriously and debated so heat-
edly by former theology are now to be understood
symbolically *only,* which is not to say that they have
no *real* meaning. Indeed, since God is beyond any
possible human conception, the *symbol* is the only
human means there is *to think* the reality of God.
The symbol, unlike the sign or the word, expresses
the reality of the experience of God without in any
way "containing" it.

But what is the reality of God? We cannot expect a definition, and the only possible approach is
through the lived experience of faith. After the Neitz-
schean revolution Tillich, like Heidegger, has turned
to an analysis of man. And, like Heidegger, he finds
the root-question to lie in man's attitude towards
his own finite, contingent, earth-bound existence.
In the face of tangled, botched, stupid chance, in
the face of human evil, in the face of history, man
can easily resign from the human race, can easily
take refuge in insanity, or in the collectivity, in the
soft, warm life of impersonal being which is lived
below the level of true authenticity and selfhood.
Where Tillich goes beyond Heidegger is in his refusal to let the question of affirming man's relation

to God remain a matter of indifference or neglect while we wait for a new revelation or for our thought to mature. Man, Tillich finds, is *unable* to face his finite situation alone. In order to achieve the courage for the anxiety which the post-Nietzschean world demands of him, man discovers, through Anxiety and Despair, an experience of *absolute faith* which gives him the *courage to be*.

"The courage to be," writes Tillich, "is rooted in the God who appears when God has disappeared in the anxiety of doubts."[26] We see now to what an extent Tillich is a theologian of the twentieth century. In this period of *Atomangst* the highest human virtue is the Nietzschean virtue of the strong man, courage. Courage is defined as

> the self-affirmation of being in spite of non-being. The power of this self-affirmation is the power of being which is effective in every act of courage. Faith is the *experience* of this power.[27]

The strength of Tillich's thought and its great attraction lie in this synthesis of Nietzsche and Kierkegaard. Faith is not the theoretical affirmation of

[26] Paul Tillich, *The Courage to Be* (New Haven, 1959), p. 190. In the interests of brevity which such a summary presentation of Tillich's thought as the following requires, I have, in the references which follow, limited myself to this book, though I have had other writings by Tillich in mind and have not hesitated to introduce phrases and ideas from them. The Tillich-scholar will know where to find this documentation, whereas for the general reader *this* book is certainly the most indispensable place to begin. *The Courage to Be* is without doubt the most important single work by Tillich from the point of view of existential analysis.

[27] *Ibid.*, p. 172; italics mine.

an uncertain truth but the existential and resolute acceptance of something which absolutely transcends ordinary human experience. It is the decision and courage to act "in-spite-of." Man is *threatened* by his finitude, by his non-being. Faith is his response to this threat. The category of Dread or Anxiety, as elaborated first of all by Heidegger and developed by the existential psychoanalysts, has also served as the basis of one of Tillich's most serious analyses of the religious need of contemporary man. The difference between Heidegger and Tillich is that, whereas Heidegger calmly accepts the *nothingness* which is in man as *definitive* of the human condition, Tillich considers it as a *threat*. Where Heidegger is resigned, Tillich is impatient. He defines Anxiety as the *threat of non-being* which pervades human existence. This threat operates on at least three levels: (1) the anxiety of fate and death, (2) the anxiety of guilt and condemnation, (3) the anxiety of doubt and meaninglessness. While the first level of man's anxiety could be resolved in a kind of stoic moralism and the second by traditional Christian theology, the third and deepest level of anxiety can only be aswered by an *absolute faith*. This is not faith in any traditional sense (faith as belief) but a power of self-affirmation through which man *is enabled* (the power is not wholly his own) to assume his responsibility for *be-ing*. The various levels of anxiety are not removed in faith; they remain and continue to be experienced, but the man of faith is free to live "in spite of" the threat of non-being.[28]

[28] *Ibid.*, pp. 40–45, 113–54. This exposition of Tillich is based on a certain interpretation and rearrangement of his thought which, while greatly simplified, does not, I think, betray it.

We can see what such a conception of religious experience and Christianity means for traditional theological theism. Tillich does not hesitate to spell out its implications. He distinguishes three kinds of theism, *all of which must be overcome*. (1) The "unspecified affirmation of God" of the pious, of politicians, of conformists, of *Das Man* in general is, of course, rejected in principle in *any* theology.[29] Besides being irrelevant, superficial, and unworthy, it is destructive of any truly religious attitude or experience. (2) The theism of theologians, of theological systems, of the *science* of God as a being among beings, albeit the "highest being," must be rejected not only because it belongs to the age of Greek metaphysics but because it is "wrong."[30] (3) Finally the theism of the divine-human encounter with God "in person" as we have it recounted in the sacred history of the Old and New Testaments, in early Protestant theology, and in mysticism must also be overcome. This last is not wrong but incomplete; its value lies in its *symbolic* rather than its *existential* meaning.[31]

When all these "theisms" have been rejected, the Christian is free to be an a-theist.[32] The question is

[29] *Ibid.*, pp. 182 ff. It is impossible to resist the temptation here of quoting a statement by former President Dwight Eisenhower as given in Will Herberg, *Protestant, Catholic and Jew* (New York, 1960), p. 84: "Our government makes no sense unless it is founded in a deeply felt religious faith —and I don't care what it is."

[30] *Ibid.*, pp. 184 ff.

[31] *Ibid.*, pp. 183, 187 ff.

[32] The great discovery of twentieth-century theologians has been that they have had as much or more to learn from

not *whether* to be an a-theist, since the Nietzschean critique of Christianity is now recognized as a necessary propaedeutic to theology, but *where* to locate one's a-theism. Any theologian, says Tillich, who studies God as a being rather than *being-itself* justifies the atheism of the present world. Theism must be transcended in all its forms, by the courage of absolute faith, and the God that will be revealed then is *the God beyond theism, the God beyond God.*

The nagging questions which this brief exposition of Tillich's thought, which we have meant to be sympathetic, calls forth cannot be examined here. Such questions would involve asking in what sense the experience of absolute faith which he describes is still specifically *Christian.* Tillich has no doubt that it is. We have called Tillich the first post-Christian theologian; this is not a title he accepts. He organized his systematic theology around the problems of Christology, and he affirms that his thought *is* specifically and distinctively Christian. No doubt he is our most authoritative witness, since it is largely his own experience which he is describing when he writes. But for those who have not had the same experience, either because they are not yet of the twentieth century or because of a certain religious blindness, the question remains.

Moreover, and this is another way of asking the same question, is not Tillich's description of Chris-

atheists than from their colleagues and that the condemned atheist has frequently been closer to God than themselves. For another example of this discovery "that there can be faith in unbelief, piety and rectitude even in atheism," cf. Henry Duméry, "The Temptation To Do Good," in *Crosscurrents,* VI (1956), 4–32.

tian experience concentrated on a certain aspect of that experience almost to the point of excluding others? Is not the phenomenological basis of Tillich's theology too narrow? He places himself squarely within the Lutheran theology of autonomy in faith. And the new *theonomy,* which he opposes to the *heteronomy* of the traditional Protestant and Catholic Churches, is defined explicitly as the culmination and natural goal of the *autonomy* experienced by the man of faith. We are willing to grant the validity of this experience and recognize the true excellence of Tillich's description of it. But there are other sides to Christian experience—described for instance by Dostoevsky—the sides of depedence, humility, modesty, gentleness, abnegation, resignation, and the acceptance of love. Such terms and the experiences they designate do not occur frequently under the pen of Paul Tillich.[33] It is as if he found in Christian love, in Charity, only the *active* aspect, the love that *I do* or that *is done* towards me. *To love* and to accept the state of *being loved* by another are not the same thing; moreover, it is the second which is the more difficult and which causes the deepest psychological problems. This aspect of acceptance, resignation, trust, response, is not much in evidence in Tillich's view of Christianity. His the-

[33] This is also true of Heidegger's writings on which Tillich is perhaps too dependent. Psychiatrists like Ludwig Binswanger have had to modify and develop Heidegger's Daseinanalytics with the categories of Love and other *intersubjective* structures of experience. One sometimes has the feeling in reading both Heidegger and Tillich that they have neglected the phenomena of intersubjectivity in favor of the solitary, autonomous self and, to this extent, have betrayed their own intentions.

ology is an exclusively *masculine* theology; it stresses fortitude, independence, autonomy, courage to be "in-spite-of." One imagines that Tillich would heartily approve of that ancient mosaic of Christ preserved in the old Archepiscopal Palace at Ravenna in which Christ appears in the garb of a Roman Centurion brandishing his cross over his shoulder like a shillelagh, going forth to *renew* the earth in spite of itself. But this mosaic is almost unique in Christian iconography. Christ as Orpheus or Christ as the Good Shepherd are more universal symbols. And even within the authentic Lutheran tradition there is the other side to the experience of faith—namely, trust and hope. The autonomy and the freedom of the "sons of light" is based on a prior resignation and an experience of faith as *trust*. Thus it seems to us legitimate to ask whether Tillich's thought does not suffer from a certain blindness to the *total phenomenon* of the Christian experience of the world, whether its validity is not restricted because of its arbitrary phenomenological base.

Then, there remains the question of God. Tillich defines religion as *the ultimate concern for Being*. God is *Being itself*, and Christ is the *New Being* and our route of access to *Being*. But do these assertions really do justice to the complexity and richness of religious experience? Certainly it is typical of Western Christian theology to define God as Being. Traditional Christian metaphysics has been called the "metaphysics of Exodus" because it found in the prophecies of Moses the revelation of the first name of God: Being, *ipsum esse*. The medieval theologians understood Being as an *existence* in which all *beings* participated. The later Reformation theologians interpreted God as primarily *presence* to man and the world. Tillich, thanks to Heidegger, has seen the philosophical antinomies hidden within these still too "anthropomorphic" conceptions of Being. The *Being* of which Tillich writes is clearly not this kind of *existence* or *presence,* certainly not of a piece with my own experienced *be-ing,* but the Ground of existence, a *meonic Urgrund.* But since the only meaning such definitions as these can have must ultimately be derived from the religious experience which they polarize and attempt to express, are we not necessarily led back from such transcendental conceptions to the anthropomorphic imagery and symbolism of traditional Christianity? We are, Tillich admits, but we can now understand the "symbolic" character of all this traditional terminology. This is no doubt true. But if even *God as Father, God as Love, God as Word, God as God* are "symbols," the historical experience which they were meant to thematize and express is not. By clothing the problem of God in the terminology of Heidegger, and by using the word "Being" in a sense in which Heidegger himself insists it cannot be used, Tillich is able to express the *God beyond God* by a term which can be understood by no one. That such a theology is safe from the taunts and the contamination of philosophy is clear. But has it not also been purified of its coefficient of Christian experience as well? Is not this emphasis on the transcendence of God a return to the spirit of the pre-Christian theologies of Philo Judaeus and the Hellenistic Platonists? Was it not precisely this theology which required the Christian Incarnation and the "humiliation" of God himself through a descent into matter? In short, can a theology of the absence of God *ever* be a Christian theology? In the end, Tillich does not answer the problem of the absence of God and the religious alienation of modern man by a *return to experience,* not even Christian experience, but by a "Hegelian" demythologization not only of Christian history and Christian theology but of religious experience itself. But when even experience is completely "demythologized" in this way, both the philosopher and the Christian have the right to ask whether anything remains at all.

Finally, we have seen that, according to Tillich, the question of God can be answered only in a Kierkegaardian (and Nietzschean) sense. Faith is not a rational guarantee but a *way of being;* it is the courage to affirm being in the face of non-being. We may wish to grant that the *courage to be* which Tillich describes is a *religious* decision and a *religious* experience. But it is still not clear to what extent the faith which gives this courage can be claimed specifically by Christians, not only in the face of other styles of religious life but also in the face of those who call themselves "atheists" in a sense different from Tillich's.

However, the aim of this essay has not been to weigh or to evaluate either the message of Heidegger or that of Tillich. It has been limited to presenting some of their capital ideas as they attempt to express and answer the contemporary experience of the "absence of God." Heidegger and Tillich have *lived through* the Nietzschean destruction of Christianity, and it is impossible today to pose the question of the meaning of religious experience except on the basis of their testimony.

JAMES M. EDIE

VI / The Rebirth of Divine

In philosophy and religion the way of purification and creation is hard. When it is actually lived through, it involves an extreme tension in which the old must be first rejected and even annihilated that the new may appear. In the first two essays, you have read that there are rational as well as irrational elements in Christianity. In the last three, you have explored, with the guidance of able critics, the philosophies of recent and contemporary thinkers who have lived and suffered in our time. Out of this life and suffering they have successively concluded that God is dead, that he is impossible, and, finally, that he is absent from our scientific and technological world of the twentieth century. There can be little doubt that these statements are the expression of a profound transition in the life and thought of our Western culture which has been widely and half-consciously shared by many, but which has been brought into the light of the word and consciously lived through by a perceptive few.

Let us now try to reflect about this experience. Can we take all these statements at their face value, or must we seek for a deeper meaning? Who is this God who is said to have died, to be impossible, and now to be absent? How can these statements be fitted together? What is their underlying sense?

ATHENS AND JERUSALEM

The basic ethos of a culture is expressed in its religion. Hence these questions raise issues concerning our Western culture as a whole and the strange tension between two opposed influences which has marked its history for the past two thousand years. In geographic terms, we may speak of this as the tension between Athens and Jerusalem, the former standing for clarity of vision, science, and contemplation of the world of objects, the latter for mystery, faith, and action in the world of life. Until very recently, the dominant values around which our Western versions of the world have been organized —our religious faith, our ethical attitudes, and our feeling for life and death—have come from Jerusalem. Our ways of understanding and our interest in nature, our philosophy, science, and technology have come from Athens.

From the standpoint of Jerusalem, there is a place, though a subordinate one, for rational understanding and what we now call technology. The life that we live on the earth is important. Man was created in the image of God to have dominion over all the other animals and to subdue the earth (Genesis I, 28–30). Therefore it is right for him to master nature, provided he uses this power to maintain himself in existence and to achieve more important ends. Our intellectual history, therefore, has been marked by constant attempts to synthesize the two worlds. One of the most important of these we have examined in Chapter II.

But in this case, as in so many others, the synthesis proceeds from a rationalistic point of view, and in the last analysis it is the historical life-world that is assimilated into the horizon of reason and explained by its causal categories rather than the reverse. This is true not only of the system of Aquinas but of the great modern synthesis of Hegel as well. These great syntheses and many lesser ones have all eventually broken down and disintegrated, leaving the two worlds, and the opposed cultural attitudes clustered around them, in constant tension and conflict. Thus at the present time, the feeling of our common language tends to oppose logic versus life, science versus religion, and faith versus reason.

The meaning of this opposition may be clarified by the distinction between what we may call *primary thinking* and *secondary reflection*. It is, of course, a mistake to believe that we live our lives unconsciously without any thoughtful guidance, though philosophers have sometimes written as though this were true. We have a feeling-understanding of what we are doing in the very act, and our lives are guided by patterns of world-meaning which have been worked out in the history of our culture and which are often only dimly understood and expressed in dramatic pictures or images. In a culture like our own where there is some respect for humanistic education and freedom, the individual person may be led to reflect upon these guiding images, to modify them by working out a way of life and a way of understanding of his own.

While this process of achieving what we call *responsibility* may be stimulated and clarified by self-conscious, secondary reflection in calm moments, it must also involve another mode of primary thinking that attends our very acts and the decisions from which they grow. Such thinking is not necessarily clear and self-conscious; it is fused with our purposive activities and works with them as we eat our meals, cross the street on our way, talk with our friends, and even as we sleep, in and through the semi-conscious little choices that guide our everyday existence. Such primary thinking is often below the level of clear consciousness, fused with feeling and action, spontaneous, original, and even creative. Kierkegaard and Nietzsche understood this mode of thinking which first worked out the great religious answers to the basic questions of life. But when left without criticism, these answers become incoherent, provincial, and closed.

On the other hand, we all know what it is to sit down in a calm moment to reflect upon decisions that have been made in the heat of crisis and upon the patterns of meaning that guided them. Since meanings always point beyond themselves to further meanings, the range of such reflection cannot be restricted to any special realm or region of life. It is philosophical in character and reaches out to the whole compass of the life-world in which we exist. Secondary reflection of this kind has been judged to be of such importance in the West that, from the time of the Greeks, a special group of professionals has been set aside to care for the primary thinking that is a necessary part of every human life by giving it helpful clarification and criticism.

Thus the aim of philosophy, as Socrates conceived it, was not to pursue special ends in an academic refuge apart from life and to replace the primary thinking of living men by great constructions of its own. It was rather to exercise a therapeutic function in helping the poets, the politicians, and whomever he met on the streets of Athens and in the market place, young and old, to clarify their primary thinking and to purify it from incoherence and error by careful criticism. Thus, as we all know, Socrates had no systematic doctrines of his own which he tried to infuse into the minds of those who talked with him. He tried rather to exercise a humbler maieutic function, stimulating them to think their own thoughts, but to think them through sanely and carefully, so that when they were brought into the light of the truth, they would not turn out to be maimed or monstrous productions.

But professional classes, provided with leisure, are sometimes led to forget the proper objects of their care, which come to seem uninteresting and dull, and to develop more imposing, special interests of their own. This has, in fact, often happened to philosophy in the course of our Western history. Instead of remaining close to the life-world in which they too were reflecting, instead of devoting themselves to the humbler task of criticizing the primary thinking of living men around them, philosophers have isolated themselves from life and have invented great systems of their own. They have often then defended their constructions as better than the meanings of living men, like doctors who, becoming bored with the imperfect stomachs of their patients, might devote themselves to the invention of great digestive systems which they would then be eager to inject (artificially) into the living bodies of men to correct their defects and diseases. Thus instead of studying and clarifying the logic of living thought, philosophers have sometimes invented new logics supposedly more efficient than the logic of our common speech, and instead of clarifying and criticizing the religion that has grown from the actual tribulations and agonies of their own people, they preferred to invent grand new religions of their own.

This has intensified the opposition between reason, on the one hand, including science and philosophy, and life, on the other, including primary religion, which has plagued our Western history and which, as we have noted, is found in our everyday speech. Religion is not an objective fact that can be observed and measured by the methods of reason and science. It arises from the primary thinking of our active existence in the life-world. It is a *world fact* which, if it is to be properly understood, must be understood by different categories in a different way. But until recently, these existential categories have been neglected in our Western philosophy, with the result that religion, as it is lived, has become separated from the secondary reflection of philosophy about religion. This is confirmed by a striking fact which has emerged from recent historical studies.

There are other important cultures where this separation has not taken place and where the clarifying, critical reflection of philosophy has been in close touch with the life-world and its religious orientation. Thus in India, we find a living tradition of Hindu philosophy developing with the religion of the people. Also in Buddhist countries, we find a tradition of critical, Buddhist philosophy that has constantly deepened and refined the primary thinking of the original religion. It is interesting to note that in our Western culture, until very recently, this union of critical reflection with cultural life is lacking. Greek philosophy, of course, had its special religious roots, and the Delphic Oracle, the swans who sing at the approach of death, the sacred ship sent to Delos every year, and other phases of the worship of Apollo, the God of light, are strongly marked in the life of Socrates. But after it died away, the rationalistic philosophy which it had inaugurated, proceeded independently, without any basic reorientation toward the Jewish and Christian religions that replaced it. Saint Thomas Aquinas, as we have seen, thought of himself simply as a philosopher, following in the pathway of *the* philosopher, Aristotle, and not as a Christian philosopher. In his well-known article, "Is There a Christian Philosophy"?[1] Émile Bréhier, the French historian, denied outright that there has been any Western philosophy to which the name "Christian" may be appropriately

[1] "Y a-t-il une philosophie chrétienne?" *Revue de Metaphysique et de Morale*, XXXVIII (1931), 133.

applied, and, though a few exceptions must be conceded, the thesis in general still stands after the searching criticism to which it has been subjected.

Now, the constant tension between primary thinking and secondary reflection can be fruitful. On the one hand, critical reflection can bring clarity into our lived existence and can open it up to new, creative possibilities, and, on the other, a close contact with life can make our reflection more sober and realistic. Without criticism, life tends to become incoherent, provincial, and fanatical, as we have noted. And in isolation from lived existence, reflection tends to become artificial and inhuman. Both these dangers are evident in the history of our strangely schizoid Western culture with its lived existence, on the one hand, oriented toward the Jewish or Christian faith, and its objective philosophy and science, on the other. With reference to the former danger, we may remind ourselves of the cruelties of sectarian fanaticism, interference with the freedom of scientific investigation, and the bitterness of the destructive religious wars of the seventeenth century which spread ruin and desolation throughout our civilization.

Let us now, however, focus on the second danger, that of an unrestrained rationalism remote from the active concerns and ambiguities of life. This extreme rationalism has tended to infuse its objective attitudes into religion, to soften it up, then to discount the human life-world, and finally to absorb it into an abstract system where its basic meanings and values are out of place. These tendencies have long been at work in our history, and we must bear them in mind if we are to understand the critical situation confronting us. We may consider them briefly under two major headings: first, the dilution of Western religion by the infiltration of objectivistic attitudes, which began in Roman times with the first meeting of Greek philosophy and Christian faith; second, the discounting and reduction of the life-world, which began in the seventeenth century with the coming of modern science, the last and most potent development of Greek rationalism.

THE VICTORY OF ATHENS: WESTERN RELIGION RATIONALIZED

In the first chapter of this book, Mr. Edie has shown the distinctive, existential factors that mark the thought of the Punic Fathers and that sharply distinguish it from the attitudes of Greek philosophy. As a matter of fact, this "irrationalism" is firmly grounded in the biblical literature of both the Old and the New Testaments. The facts recorded in this literature are not the objective facts of science which may be observed from a detached point of view. They are rather the meaningful world facts of a human history which cannot be revealed without human understanding and participation. Its horizon is not a fixed, cosmic order where all is governed by determinate causes. It is rather the moving world of history, filled with ambiguity and surrounded by mystery, where new meanings may be brought into being through crucial events and then may be transformed overnight. The divine source of the world is not a highest object, or thing, with properties following from his nature. He is the ultimate mystery, completely transcending the world in its entirety, who, from this radical distance, created it *ex nihilo*. He is not to be brought under human concepts and demonstrated, like a thing or object, but is rather to be encountered in history.

This history has confronted man with a radical choice, for he is radically free. He may either order his way of life and his whole world around his own desires, or he may order them around what lies beyond him, which involves self-transcendence and self-sacrifice. According to Christian understanding, the first way clearly ends in death, the second in a new world and a new life. Whichever choice we make will be attended by uncertainty and risk; for we cannot get outside ourselves and the world in which we live to observe them from a distance and then to derive them from causal principles. Here "reason" cannot guide us. This world has a different "logic" and must be understood in a different way. The choice need not be blind. There is evidence and insight which delineate these and other ways. There is also ambiguity. I am free for them all, and in the end, I must choose. If I take the selfish way, it will be through a trust and faith in myself as I already am. If I choose the other path, it will be through a trust and faith in something beyond me.

This faith is not a deficient kind of reason. Faith and reason are radically different, worlds apart. The one may direct me to true opinions about objects outside me that I can observe; the other to a way of life that is true to itself and the urge to self-transcendence. Biblical Christianity is not a set of doctrines about life. It is rather a way of life and a way of thinking in life. Those who follow it trust that it is leading them into a new world of meaning and a new way of being where they themselves and all the beings around them will be made new. These existential ideas and attitudes are certainly to be found, where Kierkegaard found them, in the biblical literature, which is written not in the abstract, technical languages of the special sciences and Greek philosophy but in the ordinary language of the life-world.

Hence in the first century, the Apostle Paul warns against philosophy and vain deceit after the "tradition of men,"[2] which he recognized as a rival religion in a "rational" disguise. This was the beginning of an age-long struggle in which the new faith tried to resist the influences coming in from the rational religion of the Greeks. On the whole, as we have seen in our examination of the great system of the thirteenth-century philosopher, Thomas Aquinas, this struggle was a losing battle, in which more and more rationalistic elements were accepted into the official doctrine of the Church as it grew in power and influence. Aquinas no longer writes in the ordinary language of daily life but in a technical language which is a Latinized version of Aristotle. His universe is no longer the historical world of the Bible but is the hierarchical cosmic order of Greek philosophy, fixed and finished for all time.

The divine source is no longer an ultimate mystery but a thing, or substance, with properties, the highest being in the cosmic order. He is still recognized as the creator of the world, but the idea of creation is now confused with that of causation, and

[2] Colossians, 2, 8.

God becomes the first cause of things, in line with the thought of Aristotle, the philosopher. Instead of transcending all our human categories, he falls under our concepts of being and cause and can be rationally demonstrated from an objective point of view by causal inferences from his effects. Instead of a way of life, Christianity now becomes a set of doctrines or propositions about God and the world, which are stated in the Creeds and accepted by the believers not on the basis of a free decision but on the basis of tradition and authority. If they say *yes* to these propositions, they are believers, no matter how they live and what their world may be.

The human mind is not regarded as an active source of meanings; it is rather the passive receiver of a timeless structure of things that has been established once and for all. As Aristotle said, human reason is determined by its formal objects, and by becoming original and creative, it only falls into delusion and error. Hence the range of human freedom is narrowly restricted to a single faculty, the will, which is able to choose between alternative means to an end that is fixed by nature and divine decree. Everything else that happens, including even these contingent choices—the savage tortures of the Inquisition and the Nazi concentration camps—falls into the general plan of the divine providence and will finally work out for the best. The humble Christian will accept the role that he has been already determined to play in this all-embracing scheme without protest. He will obey his masters. Instead of looking forward to a new world and a new being in the future, he will look backward to the original state of innocence before it was corrupted by human sin and will hope for a restoration of this natural condition. As we have noted in Chapter II, this is no longer the message of the biblical writings. It is a reduced and rationalized Christianity, not lived, but seen at a distance through the dark glass of classical philosophy.

SCIENCE AND EXISTENCE: THE REDUCTION OF THE LIFE-WORLD

The nominalism of the fourteenth and fifteenth centuries raised serious questions concerning the divine faculty of reason, which was the central conception of Greek rationalism, and other metaphysical assumptions of the Greek tradition. In its scepticism and in its emphasis on the need for exact, empirical observation, it prepared the way for the emergence of the modern sciences, which finally disposed of the claims of classical cosmology to have a foundation in exact, observable evidence. Owing to the infiltration of the earlier centuries, Greek doctrines had now been taken over by the Church, and it is important to realize that it was these Greek theories, not the existential core of Christian teaching, that were now the specific objects of this formidable attack.

The new science is interested in getting at things as they are in themselves, apart from human bias and distortion. Hence it tries to abstract from all "subjective" factors, in order to explain what can be observed from a totally detached, objective point of view. It shares this objectivist attitude with traditional rationalism, of which it is a special version and from which it has emerged in a continuous development. But this has been a genuine development, introducing certain new and distinctive features. What we now call *science* differs from Greek philosophical science in restricting itself to mathematical and quantitative, explanatory theories, in freeing itself, so far as possible, from any dubious, metaphysical assumptions, and in checking all theories by exact observation and measurement.

The application of this method to astronomical and physical objects soon proved the falsity of the cosy, earth-centered cosmology which had been developed by Greek science and taken over by the Church. The Aristotelian theory that the motions of falling bodies, and other physical changes, were governed by fixed, substantial natures, or forms, was also decisively disproven. These results cast serious doubt on Aristotle's hylomorphic conception of change and on his doctrine that nothing could move itself, which lay at the root of his whole theory of causation. Instead of occupying a stable earth at the center of a small system of bodies completely dependent on the rule of a divine emperor, men suddenly found that their moving earth was surrounded by innumerable, changing stars in a possibly infinite space. The self-motion of matter was later confirmed in the nineteenth century by the evidence supporting Darwin's hypothesis that the biological species, which Aristotle had supposed to be fixed for all time, were able to change and develop from one another. This further undermined the traditional arguments for a first cause of change, and it is no wonder that even before Darwin the astronomer Laplace, when asked about the existence of

God, replied that he had no need of any such hypothesis. Science has no access to transcendence. It is not interested in mysteries, only in problems that can be solved.

These theoretical discoveries in physics and astronomy were followed by technological developments which have revolutionized our daily lives, and those in chemistry and biology by advances in medicine which have improved the general health and have now added to the normal length of life. In the course of these developments in the nineteenth century, science turned its attention to the human life-world and its history. Of course it could not take account of the existing men who made this history, for this existence is in part "subjective," and science abstracts from subjective factors. It could not understand this historical existence as it is lived from the inside, for this requires an imaginative sympathy and understanding which science does not possess. Neither could it understand this history in its own world horizon, for this is not the objective frame of science. But it could do something else.

Accepting the results of the physical and biological sciences as its stable frame, it could then examine human individuals and cultures as objects, from a detached point of view, comparing and contrasting the different "worlds" that appeared in this way and then placing them in the stable, objective frame of nature. We do not actually exist in isolated "worlds" of this sort. We exist rather in different versions which we work out, at the cost of toil and trouble in the accidents of history, and which open into *the one world* which encompasses the common field of nature, our own culture, other men and their world versions, and yet transcends them all. But from the point of view of scientific naturalism, nature is torn from its context and takes the place of the world, which is reduced to its different versions, each now fixed as a frozen system, and separated from the rest.

Since each of them is now regarded as a total world and each differs from the rest, no one of them can be true, and it is easy to treat them as "subjective" delusions and to explain them as the result of external causes, chance, and accident. This subjectivizing and relativizing of the vast, all-encompassing life-world in which we actually exist has been supported by modern developments in the theory of knowledge, which have attempted to show that the world of our immediate experience is merely a collection of sense data (plus arbitrary interpretations) contained within a subjective mind-container. These impressions are "really" caused by the scientific objects which actually surround us, and the human brain, together with its allied mechanisms.

The vast, objective universe of science is governed, on the whole, by regular laws which enable us to predict the future, to build our technology, and to exercise some control over the course of natural events. The laws governing human history have not as yet been discovered, the sciences of man being as yet in a very primitive state. But the hope is that, as they develop, we may be able to explain human "choices" and the various delusive worlds to which they give rise, to absorb them into the objective universe of science, and finally to control them, as we are now able to control many natural events. Thus we are left, on the one hand, with a vast arrray of scientific facts fitting into no purposive order and having no meaning for the life of man and, on the other, with innumerable "worlds" of meaning, each making sense to at least one individual but all being equally "subjective," in contradiction with the others, and, therefore, untrue. The Christian world, of course, is merely one of these "subjective" interpretations, or delusions, that has played a role in our pre-scientific history.

Such was the situation confronting the existential philosophers of the nineteenth century, and their later successors, who rediscovered the human world.

DYING GODS AND THE ABSENCE OF GOD

The first of these philosophers was Kierkegaard, who, as a result of his reflections on the Bible, was able to achieve certain basic insights into human existence and its modes and to inaugurate a radical criticism of the rationalized, hybrid Christianity that was prevalent in the first half of the nineteenth century. He saw that the rationalistic concept of "the subjective" was an inadequate way of referring to our actual existence, as we live it from the inside. He also saw that this existence could not be adequately understood by the objective categories of traditional philosophy, even those of Hegel, and devoted his great gifts of perception and imagination to revealing its inner freedom and its basic modes. In his studies of radically diverse ways of existing—the aesthetic, the ethical, and the religious —he showed how each of them involves a distinctive mode of understanding and a distinctive way of ordering the whole field of our experience. The last way, the religious, is oriented towards transcendence and opens into a wider horizon that can take account of the narrower ones (the aesthetic and the ethical) preceding it.

Kierkegaard's bitter criticism of the diluted mass Christianity of his time is founded on these existential insights. Human existence cannot be included in the objective universe of science. This existence cannot be properly understood from the outside as an object, but only in its being lived from the inside. The human individual is radically free to choose different ways of life, and Kierkegaard says that "the most tremendous thing that has been granted to man is: the choice, freedom."[3] But unless he finds something to which he can devote himself without qualification, he will fall into despair, the sickness unto death, of which he may be unaware. Only the divine transcendence can justify such undiluted and wholehearted devotion, but it cannot be understood, without distortion, by our human categories. Hence, from a rationalistic point of view, it is a paradox. It cannot be demonstrated by any objective proofs but must be encountered in history and accepted by a faith that involves uncertainty and risk. Such faith is much more than a rational assent to the objective truth of certain propositions. There is, of course, an aspect of understanding, but this must be "duplicated," to use Kierkegaard's term, and expressed in existence. This existential faith is not a set of doctrines about the universe and its first cause, if there is one. It is rather an arduous way of life

[3] *The Journals of Sören Kierkegaard*, ed. A. Dru (New York, 1938), No. 1051.

that is open to the free individual, making maximal use of his freedom constantly and with maximum intensity. As Mr. Earle has stated, Kierkegaard felt that the mass Christianity of his time was a casual bowing before a God made in the image of man. This kind of worship made no real difference to anyone. This God was dead.

The philosopher Nietzsche, in working out his own point of view, carried this reflective criticism of Western religion one step further. He saw that the vast ranges of objective facts uncovered by the natural sciences gave no support to the conception of an anthropomorphic Deity ruling everything in accordance with a rational plan. These facts are altogether purposeless and meaningless to man. Nor could he see any signs of a single, rational Providence in the vast chaos of humanly constituted worlds with which we are confronted in the human past. In living with this growing sense of meaninglessness, and in trying to find a non-delusive answer, Nietzsche came to see that it must be accepted. There is no divine emperor of the universe on whom we can rely to bring order out of chaos. The longing for such a divinity is a pious and pathetic delusion which soothes our anxieties and smothers the sparks of freedom.

These Christian dogmas have degraded the masses of the Western world and reduced them to a condition of slavery. Though this truth has been suppressed in the past by religious power and propaganda, history shows us that man is free to constitute worlds of his own. He alone is able to bring order out of the chaos of history. So, according to Nietzsche, it is not merely the traditional image of

God but God himself who is dead. We are now rid of this delusion, free to transcend ourselves and to build a new, singing world where, as we have heard (Chapter III), we can "live in the Great Noontide." We need not dwell further on the anti-Christian polemics of Nietzsche, for they have been well described by Mr. Earle. He has also dealt adequately with their continuation in the thought of Jean-Paul Sartre (Chapter IV).

This perceptive and original French thinker owes a great deal to Nietzsche's attacks on Western religion, as well as to those of Marx, but he has developed them further in his own way. If man has been made by a transcendent being, then he is not free. He can only bring forth what his maker has put into him. But man is not an artifact. He is free. Therefore, the divine creator does not exist. He is a convenient delusion and supports us in the bad faith by which we constantly evade our own responsibilities and find excuses for not fighting to overcome our own miseries and those of the working masses of mankind. Thus the idea of a divine *pantokrator* (ruler of all things) is a degrading illusion which has stifled human freedom and responsibility in the past. Nevertheless, it is a necessary delusion, for man is a free consciousness (*pour soi*) who has tried to rest in a positive being (*en soi*) and cannot help but project an image of this kind ahead of himself, a final divine peace in which he must hope to realize without losing himself. But this divine realization of himself is impossible. The world is not rational, and life is absurd, the constant re-engagement in a futile passion.

These same criticisms of anthropomorphic conceptions of transcendence, taken from outmoded human institutions, like monarchy and imperial rule, which stifle human freedom, have also been expressed by Christian thinkers. Thus Nicolas Berdyaev, the Russian Orthodox theologian has written as follows: "In saying that God is the master and man a slave, traditional theology follows a sociomorphic type of thought, though God and his relations to man and the world have nothing in common with these social institutions, and the humiliating category of domination is altogether inapplicable to God."[4]

Around the time when Marx made his famous statement about religion as "the opiate of the people," and before Nietzsche's attacks on Christianity as a religion of self-abasement and slavery, Charles Kingsley wrote in May, 1848: "It is our fault; we have used the Bible as if it were the special constable's handbook—an opium dose for keeping beasts of burden patient while they were being overloaded —a mere book to keep the poor in order."[5]

There is no doubt that the Western world is undergoing a profound transition in its religious orientation towards transcendence. The discovery of the human life-world and its initial exploration have led to a clearer understanding of the depth and range of human freedom. The inadequacy of concepts and images taken over by rationalistic theology has been brought into the light by both enemies and friends of Christianity. It is not surprising that certain pio-

[4] *De l'esclavage et de la liberté de l'homme* (Paris, 1946), p. 90.

[5] Quoted by Conrad Noel, *The Life of Jesus* (New York, 1938), p. xix.

neers of this revolutionary movement should confuse
the outworn symbols for what they symbolize and
should throw out the baby with the bath. Thus Nietzsche cries out that God is dead, and Sartre asserts
that God is impossible. This may be true of the God-
thing whose existence was supposed to be rationally
demonstrable by logical arguments, the great emperor in the skies who rules all things. This God *is*
dead.

These symbols are no longer efficacious. But does
this mean that men of the Western world have per-
manently lost all sense of the divine transcendence?
I do not believe that this is so.

The gods have been constantly dying in our human history. Time after time great religious systems
and institutional patterns have broken down, but
only to appear again in different forms and symbols.
As a great French philosopher has said: "The idea
of necessary Being as well as that of 'eternal matter'
and 'total man' appear prosaic to him (the philosopher) in comparison with this constant manifesting
of religious phenomena through all the stages of
world history, this continual rebirth of the divine.
. . ."[6] That this is happening once again is indicated
by Mr. Edie's account of that sense of the absence
of God which is expressed by several discerning and
sensitive religious thinkers of our time, such as Heidegger, Paul Tillich, and Simone Weil. God has withdrawn from the realm of machines and the roles
that we play in the vast apparatus which is already
beginning to envelop the life-world, standardizing

[6] Maurice Merleau-Ponty, *In Praise of Philosophy*, trans.
John Wild and James M. Edie (Evanston, 1963), p. 45.

our thought and putting our freedom to sleep. The objective concepts and images which have enabled us to build up these great systems of technology are unable to help us in understanding ourselves as responsible persons, to say nothing of transcendence, the source of our human freedom. We cannot even conceive of God in this way. So he has withdrawn, as the philosophers have seen and have said in their own peculiar way.

The same fact was seen in a different way by the Jewish writer, Simone Weil, working in a Nazi prison camp with the tortured, the sick, and the dying. She not only saw with the eye of her mind but felt with the misery of her living body the absence of God from this highly efficient achievement of our mass technology, organized for the production of death. This was not part of a divine providential scheme. This was planned by man, organized by man, and carried out by man with great success. God is absent. But a God who is absent is not dead. We have turned away in other directions. We have lost contact and lack any means of approach. For the present we must wait. But a return of God is not only possible. It may be on the way, but from a new direction and in a different style.

At this point it may be well for us to think of Merleau-Ponty's remark and to ask ourselves a question. Why is it that, through the ages, in every known culture on the earth, after ancient symbols of the divine have died, it has always returned under new forms and through new symbols? What is the reason for this constantly returning sense of the transcendent? What sort of experience is it that leads us to the sacred and the holy?

THE RESTLESSNESS OF MAN

Transcendence is certainly no scientific object or any objective theory, for it is no object, and men were aware of it long before the human sciences dawned on the scene. We do not originally approach the divine through syllogistic argument or processes of conceptual reasoning, for it falls under no human concept, and men were aware of this long before they understood any formal logic. Reason in the traditional sense and the natural sciences that it has developed have no access to transcendence. Transcendence offers us no problems that can be solved. It is rather a mystery which is faced in the life-world, where we struggle for our vital concerns and face shipwreck and death. It is a lived experience in this life-world. But what is this experience, and how is it to be identified and described?

After the idea, or intention, of transcendence has once appeared, there are, no doubt, special ways in which it may manifest itself. But we are not concerned with such special manifestations. The so-called mystical experience of union with the absolute is one of these. But we wish to find the original human experience, open to all men everywhere, which can explain the fact that this intention is never absent from any stage of the development of an advanced culture or indeed from any known culture, whether it be advanced or primitive, anywhere. We are aware of the fact that, once this intention of transcendence has dawned upon the consciousness of a tribe or people, it may be symbolized in a vast variety of different ways—by the pounding breakers of the sea, by the starry heavens at night, by volcanic eruptions, by any extraordinary appearance. But we are not interested in these. We are concerned with the original experience out of which, in the case of so many different tribes and peoples and individuals of so many different backgrounds, this sense of something radically transcending them has emerged.

If there is a common experience of transcendence to which all men have access, it must be connected with a basic and universal aspect of human existence. The intention of transcendence appears to be implicit in the purposive striving of man which underlies everything that he seriously means and struggles to achieve. Augustine pointed this out at the beginning of his *Confessions*: "Inqueatum est cor meum donec requiescat in Te."[7] Human history is the story of this restlessness, and if we examine it closely, we may come to see, following Augustine, that transcendence has been touching it from the very beginning. But human restlessness is not simple, and it must be examined in its totality in such a way as to do justice to each of its essential phases. Three of these will be recognized by any careful description.

First, there is a destructive element in this restlessness, which has separated the intention of perfection from any human system of meaning, any social order, or way of life. In special instances of all of these, lasting values have been found. But none has been able to justify its claims to the possession of ultimate value. This movement was dammed up for long periods by the fixed order of

[7] *Confessions* I, 1.

mythical communities. But in time, these mythical orders, with their absolute claims, were swept away by rational criticism. In our own history, this crucial transition occurred in the sixth and fifth centuries B.C. in ancient Greece.

In other societies, similar changes took place during roughly the same period, and history began. Time after time, this history has been interrupted by the appearance of systems of thought and life making similar, absolute claims. But no sooner have they been established than individual critics and rebels have appeared, who, by their qualifications and alterations, have finally replaced them with something different. If one asks for supporting evidence, we may point to the moving world around us, which shows that history has not stopped. It is still proceeding. The negative phase of this human restlessness is the moving spring of our history. But this is not all.

There is another phase of this restlessness which is often ignored. But it is equally evident. To those who reflect upon the scope and power of destructive criticism, it has long been clear that no human construction can withstand it. If there is any ultimate sense that can justify this history, it must transcend anything that can be comprehended or achieved by human powers. Nevertheless, no sooner has a great philosophical pattern of meaning or a great social order come crashing down than men have started again, with the hope that something has been learned, to struggle for unity by re-ordering their world in a different way. Man cannot exist with negative freedom alone. With nothing to negate, it wastes away, and life itself becomes impossible. Man is seeking a unity that lies beyond him. All he can achieve is a deficient one-in-many, which he calls order, and which soon becomes fixed and closed, until it is negated and a new beginning is made. One would think that the process might well end in a negative phase of this kind. But it has not ended. After negation and destruction, a new phase of re-ordering always begins.

We must now note a third phrase of growing self-consciousness in this restlessness. Our human awareness is first of all directed outwardly towards the objects on which our survival depends, and we are not conscious of the degree to which we are responsible for our meanings. Men believed that their meanings were communicated to them from external divinities or, after the passing of mythical life, that they were ingrained in the things around them, from which they could be assimilated by a receptive mind. But in the fullness of time, after men had witnessed the destruction of many such objective systems, together with their absolute claims, by human criticism alone, a new self-consciousness began to dawn in what we call the modern age. As we have seen, the objective gods, whispering eternal truths, turned out to be mythical constructions, and the great cosmic orders were revealed as faulty interpretations of man.

We are living now in this period of dawning self-awareness. A terrible sense of responsibility weighs us down. We know that the world has not been fixed and established. We no longer believe that the basic answers have been worked out for us and that we need only look and listen. We now see that this is only a comforting delusion. The basic answers of the past have not been divinely inspired. They have been worked out by fragile, finite men. And if new answers are to be given, we must work them out for ourselves. But in the light of what we know of human weakness and the unimpressive record of the past, what hope can we have? We are surrounded by a vast array of divergent and conflicting versions of the world, each relative to the biases and circumstances of the author. Many claim to possess the truth. But for any human construction to make such an absolute claim is to deny the lessons of history. They are human, all too human.

So, like a growing child first becoming aware of the fact that he is now on his own, we feel anxious and lonely. God is dead; we must make our own way without help; but who are we! So life is meaningless. This is one prevalent interpretation. But is it the soundest way of fitting the facts that we have just noted together? In general, we may say that there are three different ways of reading this evidence. The first is the one we have just suggested, leading to a conclusion of absurdity. Let us now examine them briefly one by one, as though they were three ways of joining the pieces of a jigsaw puzzle. Which of them comes closest to fitting all the pieces together into a meaningful whole?

THE PRESENCE OF TRANSCENDENCE: THREE INTERPRETATIONS

According to the interpretation we have just suggested, there is no transcendence, or absolute, of any kind. The story of man is a purely human history. He is a restless animal who simply devours his own creations when they get in his way, as certain insects devour parts of their own bodies when under attack. Man constructs his own world interpretations, and one is as arbitrary as another. Nothing can really be learned from this history. Man is a meaningless passion, and life is absurd.

This interpretation certainly does justice to the third fact we have mentioned, the increasing awareness of human responsibility, which is one reason for its prevalence in our time. It can even take account fairly well of the negative element in history, the first fact mentioned, as long as there is some human construction to destroy. But with the second, we run into difficulty. Why is it that new constructions are constantly made and remade with the feeling that nothing is learned in the process and that they must suffer the same fate in the end? This does not make sense. It is, no doubt, true to judge such a process, if it were to happen, as absurd. But in the light of what standard do we make this judgment? We seem to be saying that the world is not rational and coherent. But why should it be? Come what may, it should be rational! Is this a surreptitious absolute? One of a very human kind?

Let us turn to the second possibility, which has been defended by great modern philosophers and is still dominant in what we call the world of the East. According to this view, most fully developed in Hegel, which we shall call immanentism, there is something transcending man. But this great spiritual power, or direction of physical force, is not merely present in history. It is inherent in, and constantly working in, human history. It is merged with man as it works out its ultimate meaning in and through the events of world history. Let us now see how it fits with the facts we have noted.

The first is the negative element which turns our achievements into dust and ashes, which shows every human interpretation to be deficient, and which leads us to recognize that no human construction or achievement of the future, no matter how great and far-ranging it may be, will prove to be adequate and without blemish. Immanentism dulls the cutting edge of this critical factor, for no matter how deficient a historic achievement may be, since the divine element in man has had a hand in its production, it has some final truth. Hence there is no place for a radical scepticism concerning the things of man. Nevertheless this view does give a lucid, though somewhat diluted, account of the restlessness which is manifest in the first two facts we have indicated. Until the dialectic process completes itself, every human pattern is destroyed but then taken up in a new re-ordering of the world, in which old mistakes are avoided and something better appears on the stage of history. This inevitable progress must continue until the final end is attained.

These first two pieces fit fairly well into this immanentist interpretation. But with the third we are once again confronted with a difficulty. What of the growing self-consciousness of man as a contingent, finite being? What of his responsibility for the deficient world interpretations of this strictly human history—for its torture chambers and gas ovens, for its miseries and agonies, as well as for its slender achievements, such as they are? What of this feeling of being alone and yet loaded with terrible responsibilities, which is such a marked feature of our modern history? What of the death of God, and his absence? These facts cannot be readily fitted into the immanentist interpretation.

Man is not strictly finite; he is also divine. As strictly finite, he is not fully responsible for anything. Furthermore, immanentism holds that the gas chambers at Belsen are not simply hideous, as they seem. They seem so only from a partial point of view. As our traditional theories of divine providence have rightly maintained, they will ultimately find a justifiable place in the great scheme of meaning that is working itself out in a more than human history. There is no account of the death of God in Hegel. God cannot die, for he is at work, even at Ausschwitz and Belsen. He cannot be absent, for he is ever present in the heart of man—bone of his bone and flesh of his flesh.

This is what the immanentist says. But in our situation, in the here and now, it is hard for us to accept this attitude, for we know that we are responsible, and we have experienced the death of God. So let us turn to the third alternative.

To us it is as yet strange and unfamiliar. So let us not try to name it. According to this way of understanding, there is something radically transcending us and separated from us, which is nevertheless both present in and absent from our history. When present, however, it never merges with man but rather maintains a certain distance. From this distance, it may excite men and lure them on to acts of self-transcendence without interfering with their freedom and responsibility, nay, rather eliciting and strengthening these, if man will listen to the call.

But whether he listens or not, it is up to him, for he is responsible. Let us now see how this interpretation fits the facts that we have noted.

The negative factor which is the moving spring of our history can now be interpreted in a radical sense. No human system of meanings can ever express the divine transcendence which has been present with and absent from us from the beginning, for this is a mystery beyond all our concepts and categories. No human institution or social pattern can express the unity we are really seeking, for this is a strict unity, beyond any order of one-in-many. No human achievement or satisfaction can realize or express this unqualified perfection. Before this, our greatest successes become as nothing, and our deepest happiness turns bitter to the taste. Furthermore, in the light of this transcendence, we may know that this will hold true not only of the satisfactions that have been achieved but of any achievement or satisfaction that ever will be achieved, from now until the end of history.

No pattern of meaning, no social organization, no individual accomplishment can stand the strain of being absolutized as though it were *the end*, which lies beyond all ends. Absolute reason, absolute sex, even absolute freedom become ludicrous and absurd. Like a deep-sea fish, they explode and disintegrate when brought to the daylight surface. And yet, while criticism and destruction are essential, they are not sufficient. The category of nothingness may lead us closer to this mystery than that of being. But it lies beyond all our categories, including both being and nothingness. Furthermore, it is semi-consciously present and touching us, never forcing but luring us on, fascinating as well as terrifying us. So after the destruction of our greatest works, in spite of this, we begin again.

In the light of our third hypothesis, we can now account for this strange fact, without accepting an absurd myth of Sisyphus. The mysterious is not the same as the absurd. It is inexhaustible and cannot be comprehended. But it can be recognized and penetrated to various degrees. Something can be learned in and through the process of world-formation, which constitutes the core of our human history. In the imperfect forms to which we have access, freedom and order seem to be opposed. Our finite freedom destroys order, and our finite institutions and organizations stifle freedom. Yet we know that we must have both to exist in a human way. Without freedom, our action becomes repetitive and lethargic; and without order, we cannot act at all. Hence ways of life that are either closed or incoherent separate us from both freedom and transcendence.

But the passage from a world horizon that is closed, incomplete, and incoherent to one that is more open, more inclusive, and more unified points us towards that ultimate source of existence and meaning in which unlimited creative power is joined with unqualified unity. One who has lived through such a transition has directly experienced the presence and the lure of the transcendent, though he may not understand its meaning. Such participation in the life of the spirit, as we may call it, is open to every living man, and careful reflection can bring its meaning into the light. There are no rational, conceptual arguments for the divine transcendence, for we cannot catch it by our human concepts and manipulate it by our arguments. But a different and far more persuasive "argument" is to be found in those critical transformations that constitute the turning points of our history.

Lessons can be learned from history. Advances have been made. But these advances are not automatic and inevitable. Instead of moving freely and self-consciously toward transcendence, we may move away and hide ourselves from it by locking ourselves in objective worlds of our own construction. We are alone in our weakness and finitude. Yet we alone are responsible for the global ordering of our world. We are on our own, and if we fail, there are no excuses. We are living in a time which has long been moving away from self-conscious freedom and transcendence. Our objective categories and habits of thought have been forged for the control of things, and for this they are sufficient. But they do not even enable us to penetrate into our own existence, to say nothing of the sacred and transcendent. So we have experienced the death of God for us, or at best we recognize him only as absent.

These facts fit into our third interpretation, which also gives us an answer to our question about the revival of religion among so many different peoples and cultures throughout the whole course of our history, after human symbols, absolutistic interpretations, and authoritarian organizations have been completely destroyed and swept aside. If this has happened before, and it certainly has, it may happen again. It is said that God is absent. Can he return again? It is said that we are living in a post-Christian era. Perhaps this is true. But can our Western religion be revived?

RELIGIOUS REVIVAL AND PURIFICATION

Without assuming the role of a prophet, I believe that the sober historian should answer these questions in the affirmative. But if he does so, without specifying any particular time, I believe that he should go on to make the following qualifying remarks. God has been absent before. In the light of the history of religions, if he returns in a time not too remote from our own, he will return in a very different form. Or, speaking in terms of our Western religious faith, if Christianity is to be revived, it will reappear with very different symbols and attitudes. This is not impossible, for our Western faith has undergone several revivals and has shown itself to be capable of basic reformation and growth. I believe that it is now undergoing a radical transformation and purification. In the light of recent events, of revolutionary developments in our existential understanding which we have reviewed, and of our present situation in world history, it is fair to say that if our Western faith survives, it will manifest itself in very different and non-traditional ways which may be summarized as follows.

Such a faith will be purified of those anthropomorphic dilutions of the divine transcendence as well as those deifications of human powers and virtues which have marked traditional thought in the past. This does not mean that the manifestation of the divine in history will be ruled out *a priori* as impossible. As it is said, with God all things are possible. But if any such revelation has taken place, it has been on the divine, not on any human, initiative. There will be no more dialectical justifications of the infinite in the finite—no more talk of a divine reason or of any divine or semi-divine powers in man. Everything in man, including his reason, is finite and human, all too human, and the infinite radically transcends him. There can be no pantheistic mixture or confusion of the two.

But man is open to the lure of transcendence, not through his reason, his will, or any single aspect of his nature. As we have indicated, the evidence for this openness is found in the restlessness that lies at the core of our human history. This restlessness not only takes him beyond any fixed human ordering of the world but also draws him toward the transcendent unity he can always more closely approximate but never finally achieve. He is free to become inhuman and to inflict untold agonies and even annihilation upon himself and others. He is also free to recognize his guilt, to take it over responsibly, and to organize a more human world. But whichever way he chooses, he is responsible, for he has power over the non-living and living things of nature. He can communicate with his fellows and is free to interpret and order things as he wishes. No one will do this for him. Hence the traditional conception of a divine plan to which he can attribute his evil intentions and vicious mistakes will have to go. These divine plans are comforting constructions of his own, to relieve him of responsibility. They are bad excuses which have now lost their power. If there is any divine plan, it is that man should become free and responsible. If he does not do so, he is to blame, and in his heart he knows this. God is not responsible for Hiroshima, Buchenwald, and Auschwitz.

If Christianity is to survive after Kierkegaard, it must be understood not so much as a set of doctrines, or propositions to be believed by an inactive intellect, but rather as a way of existing and understanding the world, with trust in the unlimited freedom and inexhaustible meaning of a creative source that is present, though concealed, in our human history. This trust in transcendence can help us to transcend ourselves and the fixed rules and meanings into which our lives are constantly crystallizing. It is beyond all codes and explanations. We need new concepts and patterns of meaning to clarify it, but there is no living culture which is wholly oblivious to its creative style of action. It enables men to break through the endless round of hatred and revenge, into which our social life is ceaselessly falling, by acts of forgiveness through which they are able to transcend the past and to begin again. By stirring up feelings of remorse and real repentance, it enables the individual person to face his own guilty past from a distance and to embark on a new course.

This way can be demonstrated neither by detached observation nor by shrewd calculation alone. It requires daring and risk, an accurate understanding of the facts, as well as the creation of new patterns of meaning. The trust in a mysterious energy which may be revealing itself through him, the trusting one, may take over his guilty past, may take over the whole situation around him just as it is and give it new meaning by generous action. Taking account of prevailing standards and accepted points of view, he will nevertheless not accept them as they stand. Without brooding over the risks and dangers to his present interests, he will, not slavishly, but joyfully,

cast his bread upon the waters, in the hope of helping to inaugurate a different world in which all
things will become new.

God may have died in the mass culture of the
nineteenth century. He may now be absent from us,
as he has been absent before. But as he has returned
in the past, so he may return again, but now making
use of new images and new symbols.

JOHN WILD